LISTENING FOR LITERACY

Early Phonemic Awareness Activities for Young Children

Aileen Lau-Dickinson, Ed.D.
Gail Raymond, Ph.D.
Assisted by Felicia Smithey

LOVE PUBLISHING COMPANY
Denver • London • Sydney

Published by Love Publishing Company
Denver, Colorado 80222

All rights reserved. No part of this publication may be reproduced, stored in a retrieval system, or transmitted in any form or by any means, electronic, mechanical, recording, or otherwise, without the prior written permission of the publisher.

Library of Congress Card Catalog Number 2001092822

Copyright © 2002 by Love Publishing Company
Printed in the U.S.A.
ISBN 0-89108-286-7

Contents

Introduction   1

    1   /P/ as in Pig   7
    2   /B/ as in Bird   15
    3   /M/ as in Monkey   23
    4   /T/ as in Turtle   31
    5   /D/ as in Dog   39
    6   /K/ as in Kangaroo   47
    7   /G/ as in Goat   55
    8   /F/ as in Fish   63
    9   /S/ as in Seal   71
   10 /Z./ as in Zebra   79
   11 /V/ as in Vixen   87
   12 /TH/ as in Thumpy   95
   13 /SH/ as in Sheep   103
   14 /CH/ as in Chicken   111
   15 /J/ as in Jellyfish   119
   16 /N/ as in Newt   127
   17 /L/ as in Lion   135
   18 /R/ as in Rabbit   143
   19 /Y/ as in Yak   151
   20 /W/ as in Walrus   159
   21 /H/ as in Hippo   167

Appendix A: Activities to Reinforce Phonemic Awareness   175
Appendix B: Phonetic Symbols and Classifications of
                American English Consonants and Vowels   179
Appendix C: Sound Associations for Creating Sound Personalities and
                Irvine Unified School District Family Literacy Project   183

Websites   185
References   187

Introduction

Learning to read is a complex process and can only be accomplished when a child has been introduced to phonological processes as early as 4 or 5 years old. The emphasis on listening skills at an early age will result in increased auditory awareness for the sounds of the language, thus forming the foundation for early literacy skills.

This manual is a resource for preschool programs. It provides activities that can be used to help young children become aware of phonemes in words using onset rime, rhyme, sound production, blending and segmentation activities. At the end of each section, suggestions for parents are included.

PHONOLOGICAL & PHONEMIC AWARENESS

Phonological awareness involves the auditory and oral manipulation of phonemes (Chard & Dickson, 1990). The most sophisticated level of phonological awareness is the knowledge that words are comprised of individual phonemes and blended together to make a meaningful word. Phonemes are the smallest unit of sound and are the basic building blocks for oral language and for the development of beginning literacy. The child's ability to segment, blend, and change phonemes within words is essential to future decoding skills.

Phonological awareness in kindergarten is an early predictor of later success in reading (Ehri & Wilce, 1980, 1985; Liberman et al., 1974; Perfetti, Beck, Bell, & Hughes,

1987). According to a study conducted by the National Research Council (NRC) of the National Academy of Sciences:

> Early studies show a strong association between a child's ability to read and the ability to segment words into phonemes. Dozens of subsequent studies have confirmed that there is a close relationship between phonemic awareness and reading ability, not just in the early grades but throughout the school years. The performance of kindergartners on tests of phonological awareness is a strong predictor of their further reading achievement. (Snow et al., 1998)

Children who have been immersed in a preliteracy environment based on phonological awareness approaches will be ready for beginning reading and early word decoding skills: (1) words can be spoken or written (2) print corresponds to speech (3) words are composed of phonemes.

Ball and Blachman (1988) indicate that most kindergarten reading-readiness programs do not incorporate systematic phoneme awareness activities in their reading programs (Strickland & Cullinan, 1990). This manual attempts to offer the teacher a systematic program to introduce phonemes to young preschool children.

INSTRUCTIONAL GUIDELINES FOR PLANNING PHONEMIC AWARENESS ACTIVITIES

PROGRAM SEQUENCE

1. Phonemic Production: Oral production of phonemes
2. Rhyme
3. Auditory Discrimination
4. Initial Sounds: Onset rime
5. Blending
6. Segmentation

Phonemic Production

This manual is organized using the order of oral acquisition of phonemes. Thus, each phoneme is introduced according to the way children learn to produce phonemes orally. With each new sound, the child learns to orally produce the phoneme and then to listen for the sound in isolated words.

The sound is stressed in the initial position of words. The consonant sounds are introduced including the unvoiced and voiced cognates such as: /p/ (unvoiced) and /b/ (voiced).

According to Lewkowicz (1980), "Children should be familiarized with speech sounds in isolation before they attempt to detect sounds within words" (694). To help children understand phonemes and their production, associate them with something familiar, such as /s/ phonemes sounds and the hiss of a snake.

In this resource manual, each phoneme is introduced with a sound association. A list of sound personalities has been taken from Edelen-Smith (1999). It is important that the teacher use the phoneme sounds and not letter names when doing the activities in this manual. It is also important to realize that sound phonemes may be represented by two letters, such as /ch/, /sh/, and /th/. Also, continuant sounds such as /s/, and /l/ are easier to hear than stop sounds such as /p/, /t/, and /k/. For stop sounds use rapid repetition: /k/, /k/, /k/.

The child practices the oral production of the phoneme by learning how to place the lips and tongue in relation to the palate. He also learns to hear the difference between the unvoiced and voiced production. A mirror is used to practice the production of the sound. Finally, the teacher shows the child some pictures with the sound in the initial position.

Rhyme

Rhyming is one of the earliest developing phonemic awareness skills. Rhyming occurs when the ending sounds of two or more words match; for example, /at/ in cat, fat, and rat. The initial phoneme (consonant) changes, but the final vowel plus consonant stays the same.

A vowel followed by a consonant is often called a phonogram. Examples are: ab, ad, ag, am, an, ap, at, ed, eg, ep, et, ib, idl, ig, im, in, ip, it, ix, ob, od, og, on, op, ot, ox, oy, ub, ud, ug, um, un, up, us. When initial phonemes (consonants) are added, the cvc (consonant-vowel-consonant) will rhyme. Examples are cub, club, hub, pub, rub, tub, and so on (Rub a dub, dub, three men in a tub). The influence of the vowel in each vowel-consonant combination is significant to the rhyme. Children who can recite nursery rhymes at the age of three tend to become better readers than three-year-old children who have never been introduced to nursery rhymes (Maclean, Bryant, & Bradley, 1987).

A rhyme is introduced for each of the phonemes in the program. The children listen to the rhymes, identify rhyming words, and finally generate rhyming words of their own.

Auditory Discrimination

Auditory discrimination requires the child to tell whether two words begin with the same phoneme. The words will end with the same sound combinations and may have different initial phonemes, such as moon and noon, pet and get, pig and big, will and fill, cat and fat. The teacher says, "I will say two words. If they begin with the same sound, say "yes." If they do not begin with the same sound say "no."

Initial Sound Activity

Here the teacher tells a story that is loaded with the target phoneme and then asks the children to answer questions about the story. The child learns to identify the words that have the beginning target phoneme. Each story uses an animal with a name that begins with the target phoneme. For example, the /p/ phoneme is found in the story about PENNY PIG.

Blending

Research suggests that by the end of kindergarten children should be able to demonstrate segmentation and blending. Sound blending is an essential skill (Lewkowicz, 1980; Lundberg et al., 1988; Wagner, Torgeson, Laughon, Simmons, & Bashotte, 1993). At first the child should be taught to blend the initial sound into the remainder of the word. For example, the teacher may say, "I am thinking of a word, it begins with /c/ and ends with /at/. What is the word I am thinking of?"

In this manual, the teacher will introduce words from the target sound story, using the initial sound followed by the rest of the word. This is described as onset rime. An onset is all of the sounds in a word that come before the first vowel. A rime is the first vowel in a word and all the sounds that follow. The teacher may introduce this activity by separating the initial sound in each child's name and then saying, "It starts with /b/ and ends with /ill/. Put it together and you have Bill."

Segmenting

Segmenting requires the child to separate the words in sentences, syllables in words, and phonemes in words. The goal is to help the child separate the phonemes in a word by saying them slowly. It is wise to start with two phoneme words before going on to three and four phoneme words. For example: /b/-/ee/, /a/-/t/, /p/-/ie/. This skill is vital for later spelling and decoding skills (Ball & Blachman, 1991; Juel, 1988; O'Connor & Jenkins, 1995).

In this activity the child and teacher will say each word slowly by "stretching" the word. Then, they will clap out the syllables in words from the target story. Other techniques for segmenting include tapping the desk, stomping feet, and placing blocks in a box for the number of phonemes. If this is too difficult, the child may need to count words in a sentence. The counting of phonemes in words is the higher level in segmentation.

Vowels

This manual will not introduce the vowels individually as is done with the target consonant phonemes. The vowels are embedded in rhyming words and phonograms. The child is encouraged to listen for the rhymes and tell which words rhyme.

/p/ as in PIG

CHAPTER 1

SOUND PRODUCTION

ACTIVITY 1

SKILL: Produce phoneme /p/ sound

MATERIALS: Mirror

Have the children explore the shape of their mouths and placement of their lips as they make the /p/ sound. No phonation is involved. Give each child a small hand mirror or use a large mirror to observe the production of the sound (stop plosive). Have the children feel the air coming through their lips. The /p/ phoneme makes the popcorn sound.

ACTIVITY 2

SKILL: Repeat words beginning and ending with /p/ sound

MATERIALS: None

Model whole words that begin and end in the /p/ sound, and have the children repeat them.

Words that begin with /p/ include:

pink	puppy	page
pat	pig	pass
part		

Words that end with /p/ include:

dip	clip	sap
chip	sip	slip
flip		

RHYMING

SKILL: Name two words that rhyme

MATERIALS: None

Share the following rhyme with the students. Have them listen very carefully and repeat back to you the first two lines.

> Peter, Peter, pumpkin eater,
> Had a wife and couldn't keep her.

Ask the children to tell you the two words that rhyme. (Peter and eater)

Next, have the children listen to the whole rhyme.

> Peter, Peter, pumpkin eater,
> Had a wife and couldn't keep her.
> He put her in a pumpkin shell
> And there he kept her very well. (Mother Goose)

Ask the children for two rhyming words other than Peter and eater. (shell and well)

AUDITORY DISCRIMINATION

SKILL: Discriminate the beginning sound of /p/

MATERIALS: None

Repeat the first pair of words below. Cover the mouth as the two words are pronounced. Have the students say "yes" if the words are the same, and "no" if they are not. Continue with the remaining pairs of words.

peach and beach
pig and pig
fig and pig
part and dart
pup and pup

INITIAL SOUND

ACTIVITY 1

SKILL: Discriminate beginning sound of /p/

MATERIALS: Penny Pig worksheets 1.1, 1.2

Introduce the Penny Pig story. Read the story and ask the children to follow while listening for the words that begin with the /p/ phoneme. Read each sentence from the list below, and ask the children to say the words that begin with /p/.

1. Penny Pig painted a picture. (Penny, pig, painted, picture)
2. First, she got her paints, paper and brushes. (paints, paper)
3. Next, she painted a picture of three pink pigs. (painted, picture, pink, pigs)
4. Last, she put her picture up to dry. (put, picture)

ACTIVITY 2

SKILL: Identify /p/ beginning sound in pictures and words

MATERIALS: Penny Pig worksheets 1.1, 1.2, 1.3; magazines; scissors; glue; crayons; paper

Read the Penny Pig story again, and ask the following questions:

1. What is the name of the pig in the story?
2. Name some other things that begin with the /p/ sound. (worksheet 1.3)
3. Hand out magazines and other materials. Have the students cut out /p/ beginning sound pictures and glue them on a separate sheet of paper.

BLENDING

SKILL: Blend sounds together to make a word (onset rime)

MATERIALS: None

The following are /p/ words. The words are divided into two parts: the /p/ sound and the rest of the word. Pronounce each word to the children one part at a time (repeat three times for each word), and ask them to guess the word.

P-enny	p-ut	p-aint
p-ig	p-aper	p-ink
p-icture		

SEGMENTATION

SKILL: Segment words into syllables

MATERIALS: None

Say words from the Penny Pig story and ask the children to clap one time for each words part.

Penny - 2 claps	Pig - 1 clap
Picture - 2 claps	Put - 1 clap
Paint - 1 clap	Paper - 2 claps

HOME ACTIVITY

SKILL: Identify the /p/ sound

MATERIALS: Worksheet 1.4, crayons, pencil

Parent instructs the child:

1. Take your pencil and trace the outline of Penny Pig.
2. Color the picture of Penny Pig.
3. What is this picture that begins with the /p/ sound?

/p/ as in PIG **11**

Penny Pig

WORKSHEET 1.1

PENNY PIG

Penny Pig painted a picture.
First, she got her paints, paper and brushes. Next, she painted a picture of three pink pigs.
Last, she put her picture up to dry.

/p/ as in PIG   13

WORKSHEET 1.3

/b/ as in BIRD

SOUND PRODUCTION

ACTIVITY 1

SKILL: Produce phoneme /b/ sound

MATERIALS: Mirror

The /b/ sound is produced with lips together. It is voiced. It is called a plosive (stop) sound.

Have the children explore the shape of their mouths and placement of their lips as they make the /b/ sound. Have them feel their vocal folds for the phonation. Give each child a small hand mirror to observe the production of the sound. The /b/ makes the bubble blowing sound.

ACTIVITY 2

SKILL: Repeat words beginning and ending with /b/ sound

MATERIALS: None

Model whole words that begin and end in the /b/ sound, and have the children repeat them.

Words that begin with /b/ include:

ball	bat	big
balloon	Billy	build

15

Words that end with /b/ include:

bib	jab	tub
tab	cab	rub

RHYMING

SKILL: Name two words that rhyme

MATERIALS: None

Share the following rhyme with the students. Have them listen very carefully and repeat back to you the first two lines.

> Bye, Baby, Bunting
> Daddy's gone a hunting.

Ask the children to tell you the two words that rhyme. (Bunting and hunting)

Next, have the children listen to the whole rhyme.

> Bye, Baby, Bunting
> Daddy's gone a hunting.
> Gone to get a rabbit skin
> To wrap a baby bunting in. (Mother Goose)

Ask the children for two rhyming words other than Bunting and hunting. (skin and in)

AUDITORY DISCRIMINATION

SKILL: Discriminate the beginning sound of /b/

MATERIALS: None

Repeat the first pair of words below. Cover your mouth as the two words are pronounced. Have the students say "yes" if the words are the same, and "no" if they are not. Continue with the remaining pairs.

bird and third	best and nest
Billy and Billy	bog and bog
bye and bye	

INITIAL SOUND

ACTIVITY 1

SKILL: Discriminate beginning sound of /b/

MATERIALS: Billy Bird worksheets 2.1, 2.2

Introduce the Billy Bird story. Read the story and ask the children to follow while listening for the words that begin with the /b/ phoneme. Read each sentence from the list below, and ask the children to say the words that begin with /b/.

1. Billy Bird is building a beautiful bird nest. (Billy, Bird, Building, beautiful, bird)
2. He gets sticks and string. (none)
3. Billy weaves them together to build a big nest for Betty's eggs. (Billy, build, big, Betty's)
4. When he is done, Betty lays her eggs in the nest. (Betty)

ACTIVITY 2

SKILL: Identify /b/ beginning sounds in pictures and words

MATERIALS: Billy Bird worksheets 2.1, 2.2, 2.3; magazines; scissors; glue; crayons; paper

Read the Billy Bird story again, and ask the following questions:

1. What is the name of the bird in the story?
2. Name some other things that begin with the /b/ sound. (worksheet 2.3)
3. Hand out magazines and other materials. Have the students cut out /b/ beginning sound pictures and glue them on a separate sheet of paper.

BLENDING

SKILL: Blend sounds together to make a word

MATERIALS: None

The following are /b/ words. The words are divided into two parts: the /b/ sound and the rest of the word. Pronounce each word to the children one part at a time (repeat three times for each word), and ask them to guess the word.

B-illy	b-uild	B-etty
b-ird	b-ig	

SEGMENTATION

SKILL: Segment words into syllables

MATERIALS: The Billy Bird story (worksheet 2.2)

Say words from the Billy Bird story and ask the childen to clap one time for each word part.

Billy - 2 claps	Bird - 1 clap
Build - 1 clap	Big - 1 clap
Betty - 2 claps	

HOME ACTIVITY

SKILL: Identify the /b/ sound

MATERIALS: Worksheet 2.4, crayons, pencil

Parent instructs the child:

1. Take your pencil and trace the outline of Billy Bird.
2. Color the picture of Billy Bird.
3. What is this picture that begins with the /b/ sound?

/b/ as in Bird **19**

Billy Bird

WORKSHEET 2.1

BILLY BIRD

Billy Bird is building a beautiful bird nest. He gets sticks and string. Billy weaves them together to build a big nest for Betty's eggs. When he is done, Betty lays her eggs in the nest.

WORKSHEET 2.2

/b/ as in Bird   **21**

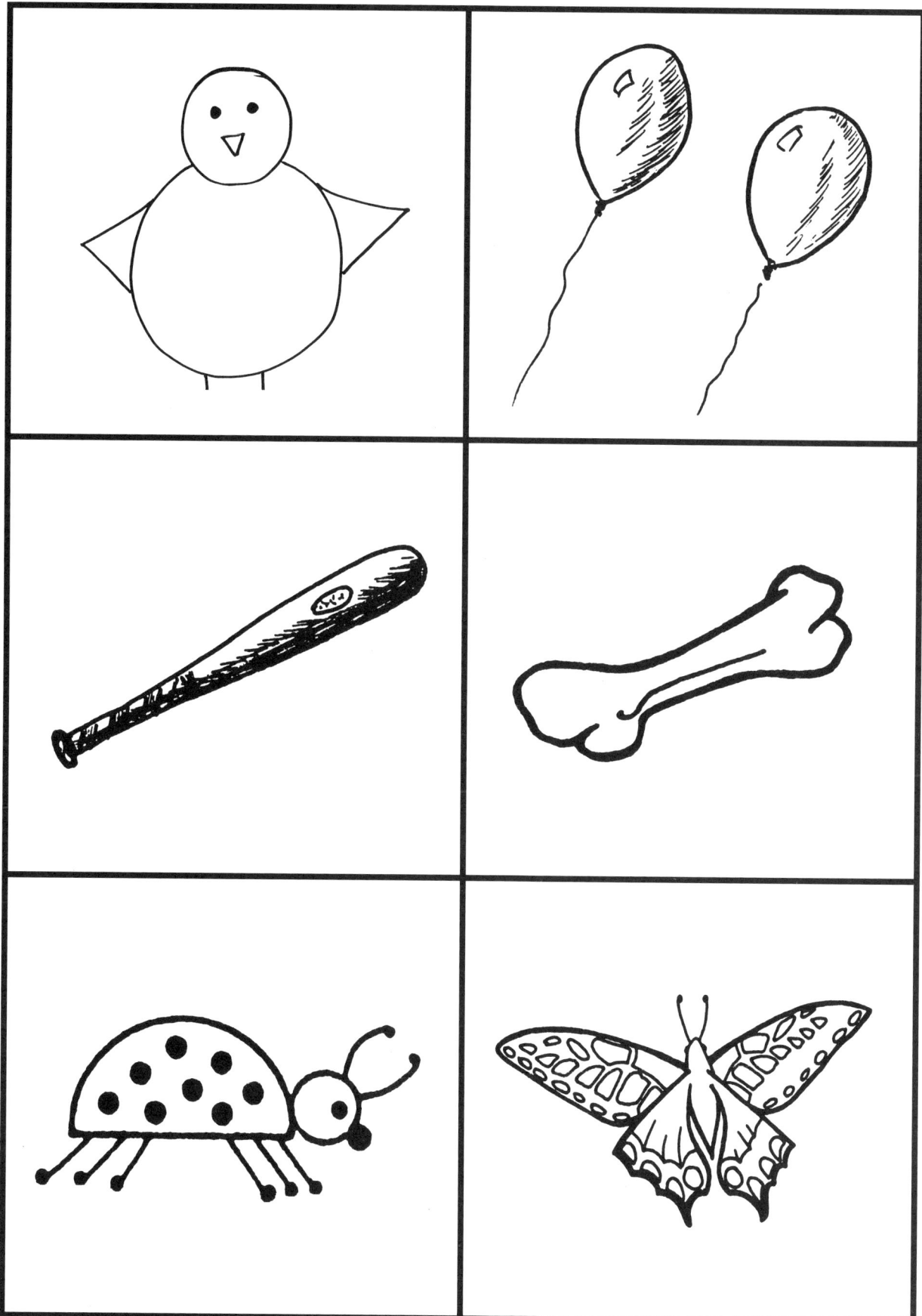

WORKSHEET 2.3

22 *Listening for Literacy*

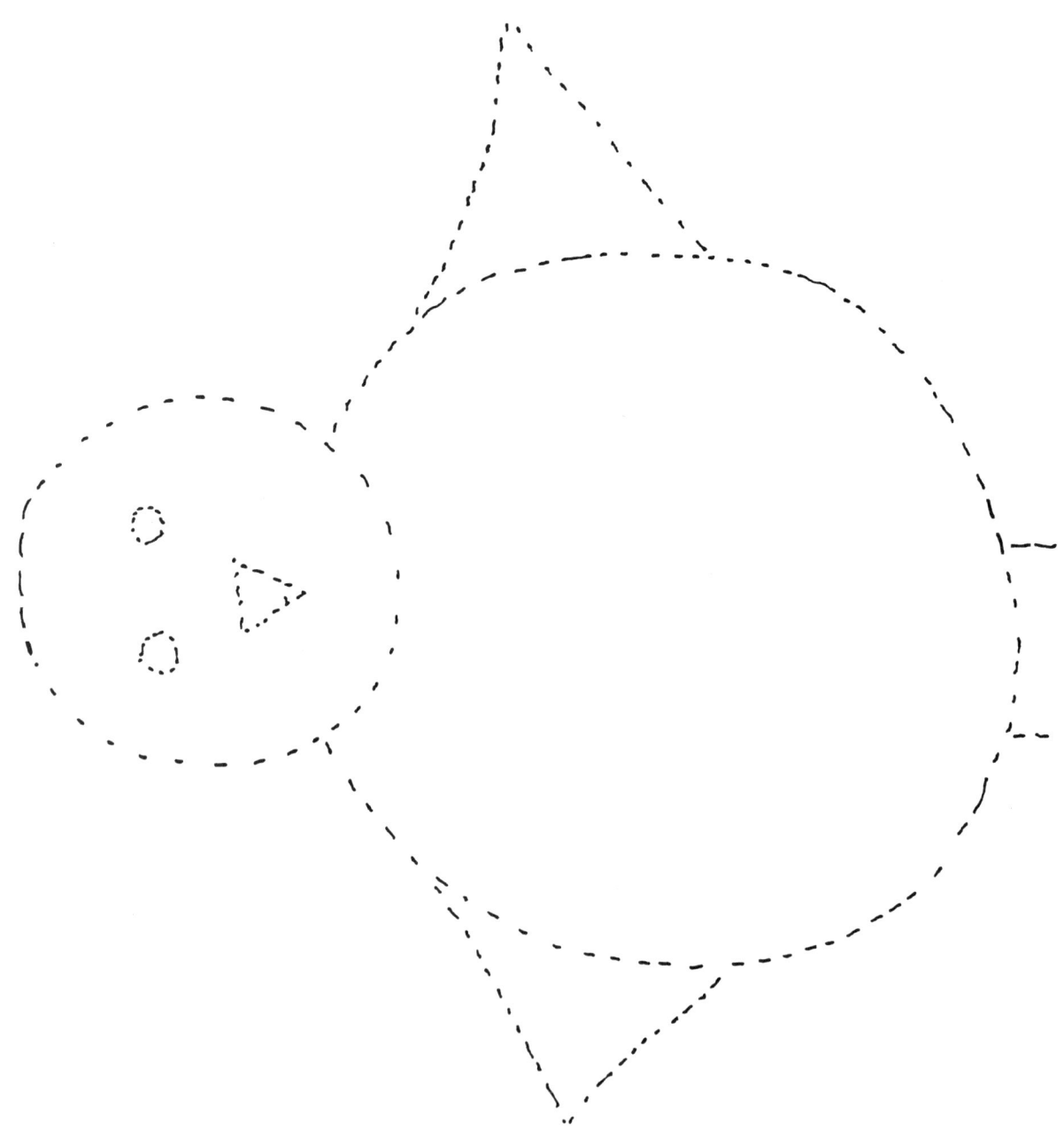

WORKSHEET 2.4

CHAPTER 3

/m/ as in MONKEY

SOUND PRODUCTION

ACTIVITY 1

SKILL: Produce phoneme /m/ sound

MATERIALS: Mirror

The /m/ sound is voiced and nasal. The lips are placed together, and breath is restricted. The /m/ sound is one of the three nasal sounds in the English language (m, n, ing). The breath travels through the nasal cavity. Vibration can be felt by touching the side of the nose with the fingertip.

Instruct the children to hum. Have them place their fingertips beside their noses and feel the air coming out. Use a mirror to observe the production of the humming sound.

ACTIVITY 2

SKILL: Repeat words beginning and ending with /m/ sound

MATERIALS: None

Model whole words that begin and end with the /m/ sound, and have the children repeat them.

Words that begin with /m/ include:

| make | man | mud |
| monkey | must | me |

Words that end with /m/ include:

worm	him	jam
ham	come	warm

RHYMING

SKILL: Name two words that rhyme

MATERIALS: None

Share the following rhyme with the students. Have them listen very carefully and repeat back to you the first four lines.

> Mary, Mary, quite contrary,
> How does your garden grow?
> With silver bells and cockle shells,
> And pretty maids all in a row. (Mother Goose)

Ask the children to tell you the two words that rhyme. (grow and row)

Next, have the children listen to the whole rhyme again.

> Mary, Mary, quite contrary,
> How does your garden grow?
> With silver bells and cockle shells,
> And pretty maids all in a row. (Mother Goose)

Ask the children for two rhyming words other than grow and row. (bells and shells)

AUDITORY DISCRIMINATION

SKILL: Discriminate the beginning sound of /m/

MATERIALS: None

Repeat the first pair of words below. Cover your mouth as the two words are pronounced. Have the students say "yes" if the words are the same, and "no" if they are not. Continue with remaining pairs.

> man and fan
> monkey and donkey

me and me
make and take
mud and mud

INITIAL SOUND

ACTIVITY 1

SKILL: Discriminate beginning sound of /m/

MATERIALS: Mandy Monkey worksheets 3.1, 3.2

Introduce the Mandy Monkey story. Read the story and ask the children to follow while listening for the words that begin with the /m/ phoneme. Read each sentence from the list below, and ask the children to say the words that begin with /m/.

1. Mandy Monkey likes to make macaroni. (Mandy, Monkey, make, macaroni)
2. First, she fills a pot of water. (none)
3. Next, she puts it on the stove. (none)
4. When the water boils Mandy puts the macaroni in the water. (Mandy, macaroni)
5. Mandy Monkey lets it cook until it is soft. (Mandy, monkey)

ACTIVITY 2

SKILL: Identify /m/ beginning sounds in pictures and words

MATERIALS: Mandy Monkey worksheets 3.1, 3.2, 3.3; magazines; scissors; glue; crayons; paper

Ask the students to remember the Mandy Monkey story, and ask the following questions.

1. What is the name of the monkey in the story?
2. Name some other things that begin with the /m/ sound. (worksheet 3.3)
3. Hand out magazines and other materials. Have the students cut out /m/ beginning sound pictures and glue them on a separate sheet of paper.

BLENDING

SKILL: Blend sounds together to make a word

MATERIALS: None

The following are /m/ words. The words are divided into two parts: the /m/ sound and the rest of the word. Pronounce each word to the children one part at a time (repeat three times for each word), and ask them to guess the word.

| M-andy | m-e | m-acaroni |
| m-ake | m-onkey | m-ud |

SEGMENTATION

SKILL: Segment words into syllables

MATERIALS: The Mandy Monkey story (worksheet 3.2)

Say words from the story and ask the children to clap one time for each word part.

Mandy - 2 claps	Make - 1 clap
Me - 1 clap	Monkey - 2 claps
Macaroni - 3 claps	Mud - 1 clap

HOME ACTIVITY

SKILL: Identify the /m/ sound

MATERIALS: Worksheet 3.4, crayons, pencil

Parent instructs the child:

1. Take your pencil and trace the outline of Mandy Monkey.
2. Color the picture of Mandy Monkey.
3. What is this picture that begins with the /m/ sound?

/m/ as in Monkey **27**

Mandy Monkey

WORKSHEET 3.1

MANDY MONKEY

Mandy **M**onkey likes to **m**ake **m**acaroni. First, she fills a pot with water. Next, she puts it on the stove. When the water boils **M**andy puts the **m**acaroni in the water. **M**andy **M**onkey lets it cook until it is soft.

WORKSHEET 3.2

/m/ as in Monkey 29

WORKSHEET 3.3

30   *Listening for Literacy*

Mandy Monkey

WORKSHEET 3.4

/t/ as in TURTLE

CHAPTER 4

SOUND PRODUCTION

ACTIVITY 1

SKILL: Produce phoneme /t/ sound

MATERIALS: Mirror

Have the children explore the shape of their mouths and placement of their lips as they make the /t/ sound. No phonation is involved. Give each child a small hand mirror to observe the production of the sound. The children should use the tip of the tongue on the ridge behind the upper teeth (stop plosive). This is an unvoiced sound. Have the children feel the air coming through the teeth. The /t/ sound makes the sound of a ticking clock.

ACTIVITY 2

SKILL: Repeat words beginning and ending with /t/ sound

MATERIALS: None

Model whole words that begin and end in the /t/ sound, and have the children repeat them.

Words that begin with /t/ include:

| top | tip | turtle |
| table | tap | toe |

Words that end with /t/ include:

bat	mat	cot
cat	fat	hot

RHYMING

SKILL: Name two words that rhyme

MATERIALS: None

Share the following rhyme with the students. Have them listen very carefully and repeat back to you the first two lines.

> Little Tommy Tucker
> Sings for his supper.

Ask the children to tell you the two words that rhyme. (Tucker and supper)

Next, have the children listen to the whole rhyme.

> Little Tommy Tucker
> Sings for his supper.
> What shall we give him.
> Brown bread and butter?
> How shall he cut it without a knife?
> How shall he marry without ere a wife? (Mother Goose)

Ask the children for two rhyming words other than Tucker and supper. (knife and wife)

AUDITORY DISCRIMINATION

SKILL: Discriminate the beginning sound of /t/

MATERIALS: None

Repeat the first pair of words below. Cover your mouth as the two words are pronounced. Have the students say "yes" if the words are the same, and "no" if they are not.

teach and beach

turtle and myrtle
trip and trip
Tucker and sucker
Tom and Tom

INITIAL SOUND

ACTIVITY 1

SKILL: Discriminate beginning sound of /t/

MATERIALS: Tommy Turtle worksheet 4.2

Introduce the Tommy Turtle story. Read the story and ask the children to follow while listening for the words that begin with the /t/ phoneme. Read each sentence from the list below, and ask the children to say the words that have the /t/ sound.

1. Tommy Turtle liked the tic-toc of a clock. (Tommy, Turtle, tic, toc)
2. He wanted to tell time. (to, tell, time)
3. He asked his teacher to teach him to tell time. (teacher, to, teach, to, tell, time)
4. She said, "Tommy Turtle, you're too tiny to tell time." (Tommy, Turtle, too, tiny, tell, time)

ACTIVITY 2

SKILL: Identify /t/ beginning sounds in pictures and words

MATERIALS: Tommy Turtle worksheets 4.1, 4.2, 4.3; magazines; scissors; glue; crayons; paper

Read the Tommy Turtle story again, and ask the following questions:

1. What is the name of the turtle in the story?
2. Name some other things that begin with the /t/ sound. (worksheet 4.3)
3. Hand out magazines and other materials. Have the students cut out /t/ beginning sound pictures and glue them on a separate sheet of paper.

BLENDING

SKILL: Blend sounds together to make a word

MATERIALS: None

The following are /t/ words. The words are divided into two parts: the /t/ sound and the rest of the word. Pronounce each word to the children one part at a time (repeat three times for each word), and ask them to guess the word.

T-ommy	t-eacher	t-ime
t-ic	t-urtle	t-o
t-oc	t-iny	t-ell

SEGMENTATION

SKILL: Segment words into syllables

MATERIALS: None

Say words from the Tommy Turtle story and ask the children to clap one time for each word part

Tommy - 2 claps	Tic - 1 clap
Toc - 1 clap	Time - 1 clap
Turtle - 2 claps	Teacher - 2 claps
Teach - 1 clap	

HOME ACTIVITY

SKILL: Identify the /t/ sound

MATERIALS: Worksheet 4.4, crayons, pencil

Parent instructs the child:

1. Take your pencil and trace the outline of Tommy Turtle.
2. Color the picture of Tommy Turtle.
3. What is this picture that begins with the /t/ sound?

/t/ as in Turtle **35**

Tommy Turtle

WORKSHEET 4.1

TOMMY TURTLE

Tommy Turtle liked the tic-toc of a clock. He wanted to tell time. He asked his teacher to teach him to tell time. She said, "Tommy Turtle, you're too tiny to tell time."

/t/ as in Turtle **37**

WORKSHEET 4.3

38 *Listening for Literacy*

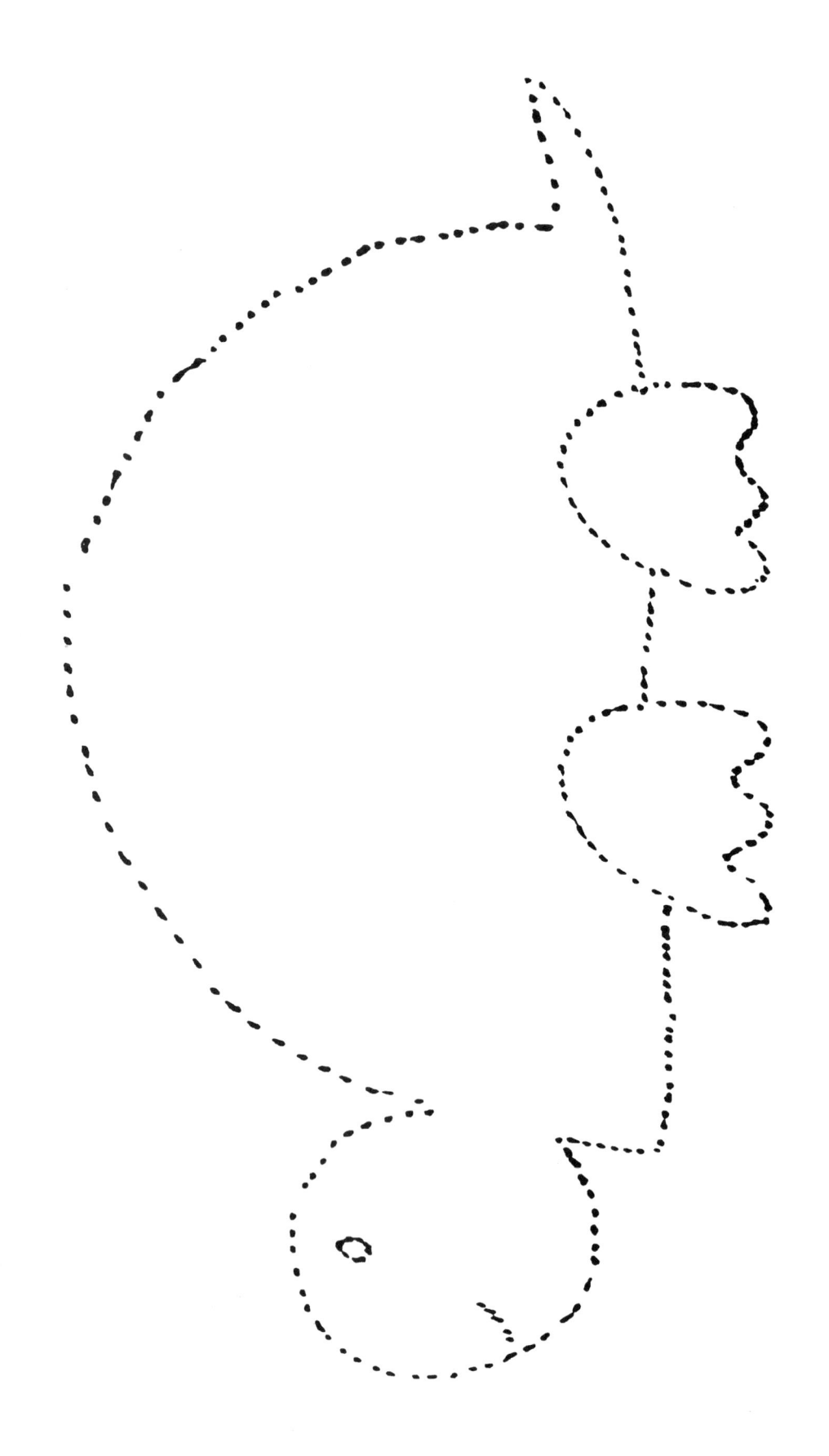

WORKSHEET 4.4

CHAPTER 5

/d/ as in DOG

SOUND PRODUCTION

ACTIVITY 1

SKILL: Produce phoneme /d/ sound

MATERIALS: Mirror

The /d/ sound is a voiced sound. It is produced by placing the tip of the tongue on the ridge behind the upper teeth (stop plosive).

Have the children explore the shape of their mouths and placement of their lips as they make the /d/ sound. Have them feel their vocal folds for the phonation. Give each child a small hand mirror or use a large mirror to observe the production of the sound. This is pecking woodpecker sound.

ACTIVITY 2

SKILL: Repeat words beginning and ending with the /d/ sound

MATERIALS: None

Model whole words that begin and end in the /d/ sound, and have the children repeat them.

Words that begin with /d/ include:

Danny	dad	draw
dog	do	duck
dig		

Words that end with /d/ include:

dad	mad	red
build	sad	bed
bud	glad	

RHYMING

SKILL: Name two words that rhyme

MATERIALS: None

Share the following rhyme with the students. Have them listen very carefully and repeat back to you the first line.

> A dillar, a dollar, a ten o'clock scholar.

Ask the children to tell you the two words that rhyme. (dollar and scholar)

Next, have the children listen to the whole rhyme.

> A dillar, a dollar, a ten o'clock scholar.
> What makes you come so soon?
> You used to come at ten o'clock,
> But now you come at noon. (Mother Goose)

Ask the children for two rhyming words other than dollar and scholar. (soon and noon)

AUDITORY DISCRIMINATION

SKILL: Discriminate the beginning sound of /d/

MATERIALS: None

Repeat the first pair of words below. Cover your mouth as the two words are pronounced. Have the students say "yes" if the words are the same, and "no" if they are not. Continue with the remaining pairs.

    ditch and ditch
    dig and big
    Dan and Dan
    day and bay
    door and poor

INITIAL SOUND

ACTIVITY 1

SKILL: Discriminate beginning sound of /d/

MATERIALS: Danny Dog worksheet 5.2

Introduce the Danny Dog story. Read the story and ask the children to follow while listening for the words that begin with the /d/ phoneme. Read each sentence from the list below, and ask the children to say the words that contain the /d/ sound.

1. Danny dog likes to dig. (Danny, dig, dog)
2. He digs holes all over the yard. (digs)
3. He digs by the door. (digs, door)
4. Danny digs by the tree. (Danny, digs)
5. Danny digs all day. (Danny, digs, day)

ACTIVITY 2

SKILL: Identify /d/ beginning sound in pictures and words

MATERIALS: Danny Dog worksheets 5.1, 5.2, 5.3; magazines; scissors; glue; crayons; paper

Read the Danny Dog story again, and ask the following questions:

1. What is the name of the dog in the story?
2. Name some other things that begin with the /d/ sound. (worksheet 5.3)
3. Hand out magazines and other materials. Have the students cut out /d/ beginning sound pictures and glue them on a separate sheet of paper.

BLENDING

SKILL: Blend sounds together to make a word

MATERIALS: None

The following are /d/ words. The words are divided into two parts: the /d/ sound and the rest of the word. Pronounce each word to the children one part at a time (repeat three times for each word), and ask them to guess the word.

D-anny	d-ig	d-ay
d-og	d-oor	

SEGMENTATION

SKILL: Segment words into syllables

MATERIALS: The Danny Dog story (worksheet 5.2)

Say /d/ words from the story and ask the children to clap one time for each word part.

Danny - 2 claps	Dog - 1 clap
Dig - 1 clap	Door - 1 clap
Day - 1 clap	

HOME ACTIVITY

SKILL: Identify the /d/ sound

MATERIALS: Worksheet 5.4, crayons, pencil

Parent instructs the child:
1. Take your pencil and trace the outline of Danny Dog.
2. Color the picture of Danny Dog.
3. What is this picture that begins with the /d/ sound?

/d/ as in Dog **43**

Danny Dog

WORKSHEET 5.1

DANNY DOG

Danny Dog likes to dig. He digs holes all over the yard. He digs by the door. Danny digs by the trees. Danny digs all day.

WORKSHEET 5.2

/d/ as in Dog   **45**

WORKSHEET 5.3

46 *Listening for Literacy*

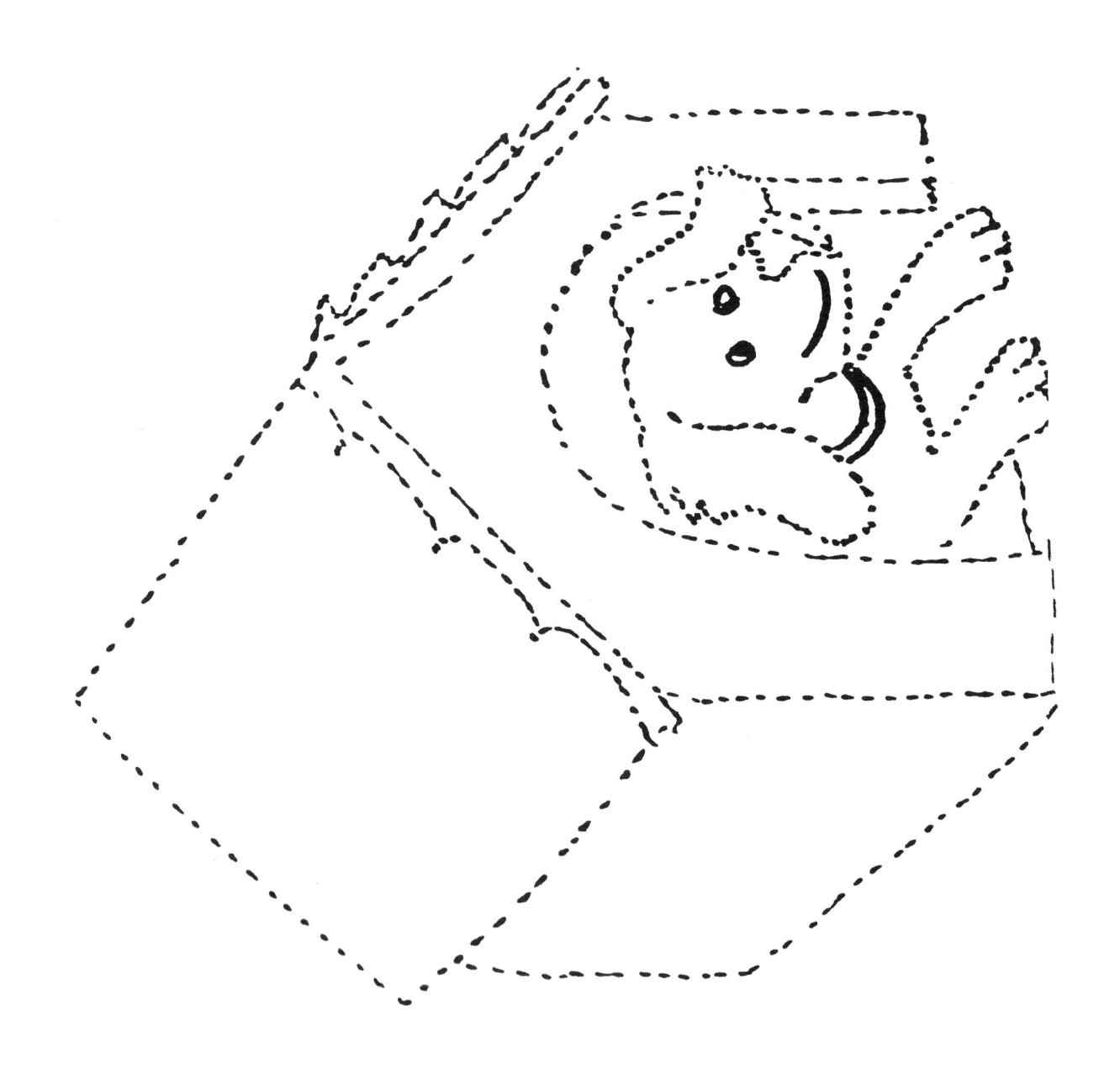

WORKSHEET 5.4

CHAPTER 6

/k/ as in KANGAROO

SOUND PRODUCTION

ACTIVITY 1

SKILL: Produce phoneme /k/ sound

MATERIALS: Mirror

The /k/ sound is produced by raising the back of the tongue, humped up to the soft palate. It is an unvoiced (breath) sound and a plosive stop sound.

Have the children explore the shape of their mouths and placement of their lips as they make the /k/ sound. Give each child a small hand mirror to observe the production of the sound. The students should feel the air escaping as the sound is produced. The /k/ makes the crow sound.

ACTIVITY 2

SKILL: Repeat words beginning and ending with /k/ sound

MATERIALS: None

Model whole words that begin and end in the /k/ sound, and have the children repeat them.

Words that begin with /k/ include:

| king | cat | kite |
| key | can | kick |

Words that end with /k/ include:

kick	mack	like
pick	book	bike
tack		

RHYMING

SKILL: Name two words that rhyme

MATERIALS: None

Share the following rhyme with the students. Have them listen very carefully and repeat back to you the first two lines.

> Old King Cole was a merry old soul,
> And a merry old soul was he;

Ask the children to tell you the two words that rhyme. (Cole and soul)

Next, have the children listen to the whole rhyme.

> Old King Cole was a merry old soul,
> And a merry old soul was he;
> He called for his pipe, and he called for his bowl,
> And he called for his fiddlers three. (Mother Goose)

Ask the children for two rhyming words other than Cole and soul. (he and three)

AUDITORY DISCRIMINATION

SKILL: Discriminate the beginning sound of /k/

MATERIALS: None

Repeat the first pair of words below. Cover your mouth as the two words are pronounced. Have the students say "yes"

if the words are the same, and "no" if they are not. Continue with remaining pairs.

> cat and cat
> Cole and soul
> Ken and Ken
> kick and lick
> king and king

INITIAL SOUND

ACTIVITY 1

SKILL: Discriminate beginning sound of /k/

MATERIALS: Katy Kangaroo worksheet 6.2

Introduce the Katy Kangaroo story. Read the story and ask the children to follow while listening for the words that begin with the /k/ phoneme. Read each sentence from the list below, and ask the children to say the words that contain the /k/ sound.

1. Katy Kangaroo kicks a ball. (Katy, Kangaroo, kicks)
2. Katy Kangaroo kicks it very high. (Katy, Kangaroo, kicks)
3. Katy Kangaroo has a yellow ball to kick. (Katy, Kangaroo, kick)
4. Katy Kangaroo kicks the ball to her friend Ken. (Katy, Kangaroo, kicks, Ken)

ACTIVITY 2

SKILL: Identify /k/ beginning sounds in pictures and words

MATERIALS: Katy Kangaroo worksheets 6.1, 6.2, 6.3; magazines; scissors; glue; crayons; paper

Read the Katy Kangaroo story again, and ask the following questions:

1. What is the name of the kangaroo in the story?
2. Name some other things that begin with the /k/ sound. (worksheet 6.3)

3. Hand out magazines and other materials. Have the students cut out /k/ beginning sound pictures and glue them on a separate sheet of paper.

BLENDING

SKILL: Blend sounds together to make a word

MATERIALS: None

The following are /k/ words. The words are divided into two parts: the /k/ sound and the rest of the word. Pronounce each word to the children one part at a time (repeat three times for each word), and ask them to guess the word.

| K-aty | k-ick | K-en |
| k-ing | k-ey | c-at |

SEGMENTATION

SKILL: Segment words into syllables

MATERIALS: The Katy Kangaroo story (worksheet 6.2)

Say /k/ words from the Katy Kangaroo story and ask children to clap one time for each word part.

| Katy - 2 claps | Kangaroo - 3 claps |
| kick - 1 clap | Ken - 1 clap |

HOME ACTIVITY

SKILL: Identify the /k/ sound

MATERIALS: Worksheet 6.4, crayons, pencil

Parent instructs the child:
1. Take your pencil and trace the outline of Katy Kangaroo.
2. Color the picture of Katy Kangaroo.
3. What is this picture that begins with the /k/ sound?

/k/ as in Kangaroo **51**

Katy Kangaroo

WORKSHEET 6.1

KATY KANGAROO

Katy Kangaroo kicks a ball. Katy Kangaroo kicks it very high. Katy Kangaroo has a yellow ball to kick. Katy Kangaroo kicks the ball to her friend Ken.

WORKSHEET 6.2

/k/ as in Kangaroo   **53**

WORKSHEET 6.3

54 *Listening for Literacy*

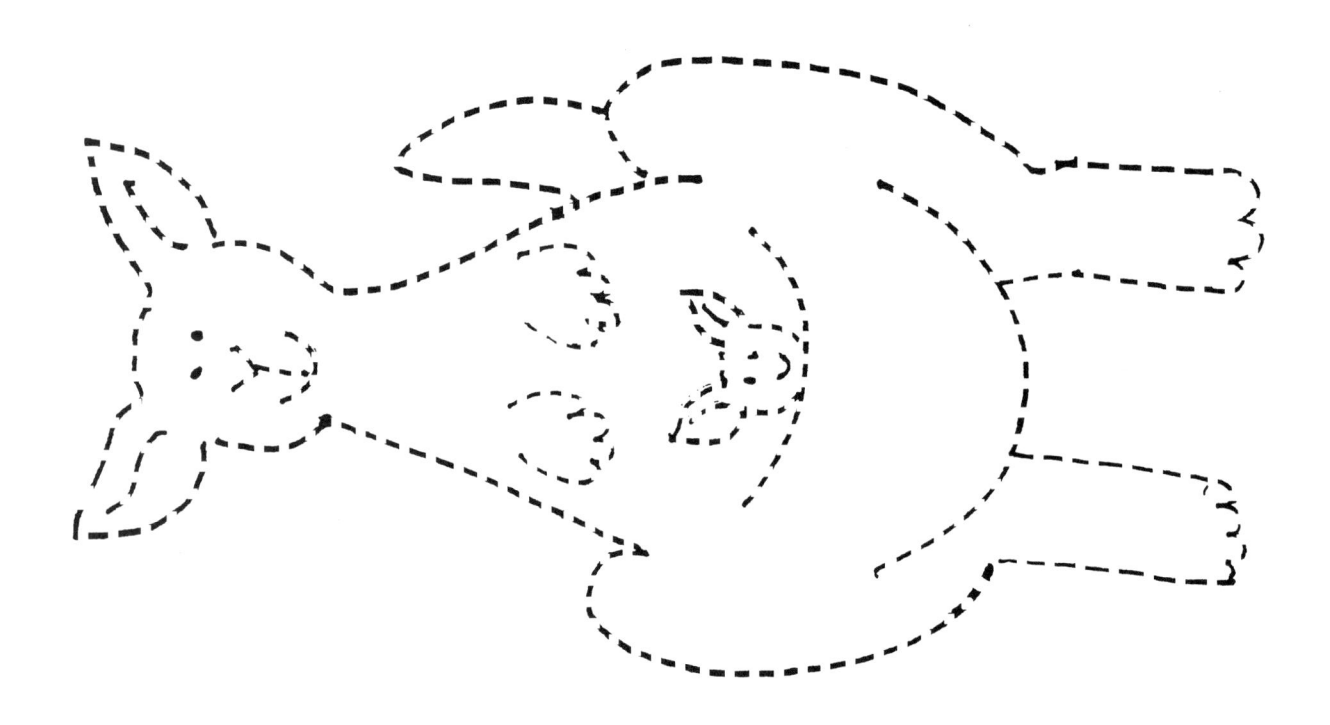

WORKSHEET 6.4

CHAPTER 7

/g/ as in GOAT

SOUND PRODUCTION

ACTIVITY 1

SKILL: Produce phoneme /g/ sound

MATERIALS: Mirror

The /g/ sound is produced by raising the back of the tongue, humped up to the soft palate. It is a voiced sound and is a plosive (stop) sound such as in go, get, and girl.

Have the children explore the shape of their mouths as they make the /g/ sound. Have them feel their vocal folds for the phonation. Give each child a small hand mirror to observe the production of the sound. The /g/ makes the gurgling sound.

ACTIVITY 2

SKILL: Repeat words beginning and ending with /g/ sound

MATERIALS: None

Model whole words that begin and end in the /g/ sound, and have the children repeat them.

Words that begin with /g/ include:

Gary	goes	get
goat	go	

Words that end with /g/ include:

bag	wag	zag
tag	gag	

RHYMING

SKILL: Name two words that rhyme

MATERIALS: None

Share the following rhyme with the students. Have them listen very carefully and repeat back to you the first two lines.

> Gobble, Gobble
> Hibble, Hobble

Ask the children to tell you the two words that rhyme. (gobble, hobble)

Next, have the children listen to the whole rhyme.

> Gobble, Gobble
> Hibble, Hobble
> Went the turkey hen
> Gobble, Gobble
> Hibble, Hobble
> Away he went down the glen. (Authors)

Ask the children for two rhyming words other than gander and wander. (hen and glen)

AUDITORY DISCRIMINATION

SKILL: Discriminate the beginning sound of /g/

MATERIALS: None

Repeat the first pair of words below. Cover your mouth as the two words are pronounced. Have the students say "yes" if the words are the same, and "no" if they are not. Continue with the remaining pairs.

> gate and date
> goat and goat

go and mo
goose and goose
get and bet

INITIAL SOUND

ACTIVITY 1

SKILL: Discriminate beginning sound of /g/

MATERIALS: Gary Goat worksheet 7.2

Introduce the Gary Goat story. Read the story and ask the children to follow while listening for the words that begin with the /g/ phoneme. Read each sentence from the list below, and ask the children to say the words that begin with /g/.

1. Gary Goat goes to the store to get a gift. (Gary, Goat, goes, get, gift)
2. He is going to give the gift to Goofy Gertie. (going, give, gift, goofy, Gertie)
3. Goofy Gertie is his girlfriend. (Goofy, Gertie, girlfriend)
4. She wants a goldfish for a gift. (goldfish, gift)

ACTIVITY 2

SKILL: Identify /g/ beginning sounds in pictures and words

MATERIALS: Gary Goat worksheets 7.1, 7.2, 7.3; magazines; scissors; glue; crayons; paper

Read the Gary Goat story again, and ask the following questions:

1. What is the name of the goat in the story?
2. Name some other things that begin with the /g/ sound. (worksheet 7.3)
3. Hand out magazines and other materials. Have the students cut out /g/ beginning sound pictures and glue them on a separate sheet of paper.

BLENDING

SKILL: Blend sounds together to make a word

MATERIALS: None

The following are /g/ words. The words are divided into two parts: the /g/ sound and the rest of the word. Pronounce each word to the children one part at a time (repeat three times for each word), and ask them to guess the word.

G-ary	G-oat	g-o
g-et	g-ift	g-oes
g-irl	g-old	g-oofy

SEGMENTATION

SKILL: Segment words into syllables

MATERIALS: The Gary Goat story (worksheet 7.2)

Say /g/ words from the story and ask children to clap one time for each word part.

Gary - 2 claps	Goat - 1 clap
Gift - 1 clap	Goofy - 2 claps
Gertie - 2 claps	Goldfish - 2 claps
Girlfriend - 2 claps	

HOME ACTIVITY

SKILL: Identify the /g/ sound

MATERIALS: Worksheet 7.4, crayons, pencil

Parent instructs the child:

1. Take your pencil and trace the outline of Gary Goat.
2. Color the picture of Gary Goat.
3. What is this picture that begins with the /g/ sound?

/g/ as in Goat   **59**

Gary Goat

WORKSHEET 7.1

GARY GOAT

Gary Goat goes to the store to get a gift. He is going to give the gift to Goofy Gertie. Goofy Gertie is his girlfriend. She wants a goldfish for a gift.

/g/ as in Goat   **61**

WORKSHEET 7.3

62   *Listening for Literacy*

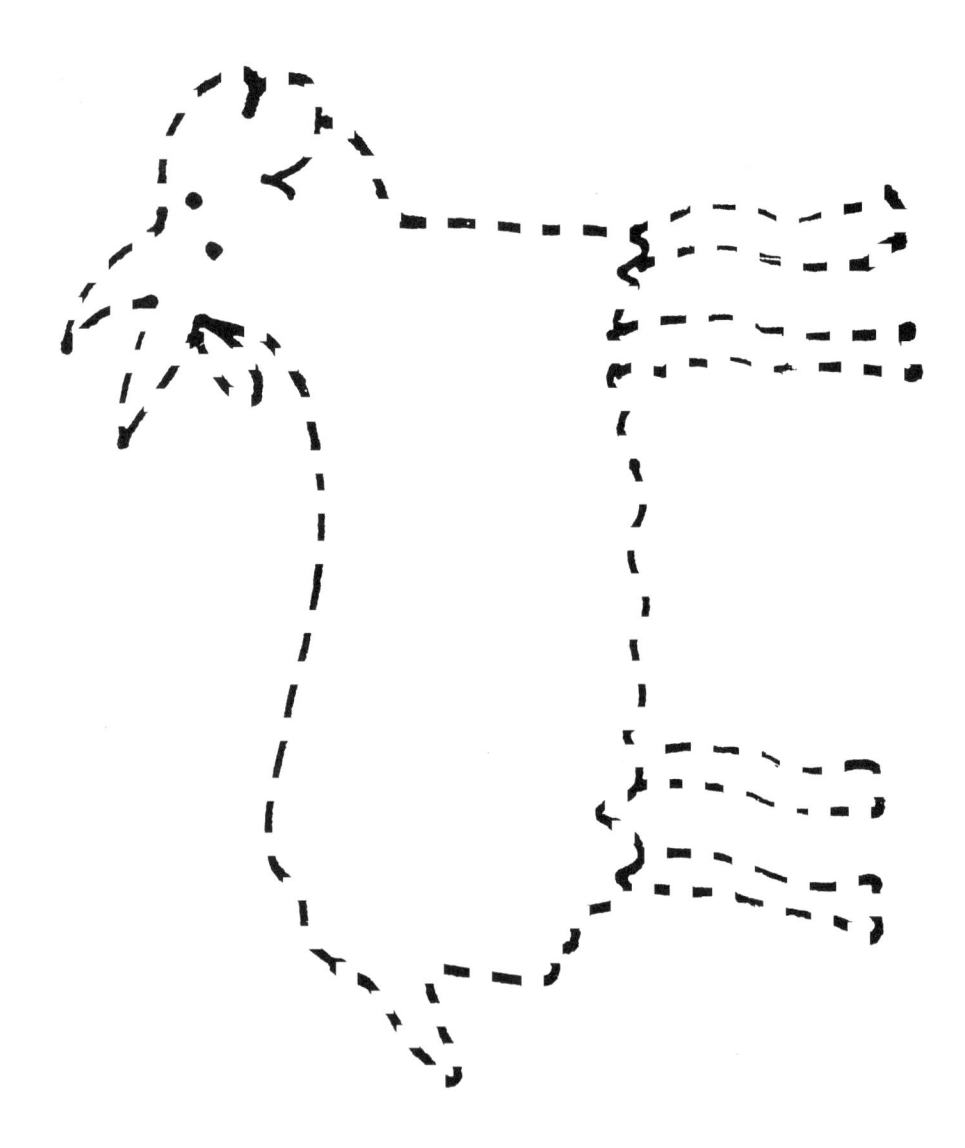

WORKSHEET 7.4

CHAPTER 8

/f/ as in FISH

SOUND PRODUCTION

ACTIVITY 1

SKILL: Produce phoneme /f/ sound

MATERIALS: Mirror

The /f/ sound is a fricative. It is an unvoiced sound. To make the sound, place the upper teeth on the lower lip. Release a steady stream of breath.

Have the children explore the shape of their mouths and placement of their lips as they make the /f/ sound. Give each child a small hand mirror to observe the production of the sound. The /f/ makes the angry cat sound.

ACTIVITY 2

SKILL: Repeat words beginning and ending with /f/ sound

MATERIALS: None

Model whole words that begin and end in the /f/ sound, and have the children repeat them.

Words that begin with /f/ include:

| fit | fig | fan |
| fat | first | friend |

63

Words that end with /f/ include:

deaf	knife	puff
leaf	muff	laugh
half	if	

RHYMING

SKILL: Name two words that rhyme

MATERIALS: None

Share the following rhyme with the students. Have them listen very carefully and repeat back to you the first two lines.

> Fiddle-de-dee, fiddle-de-dee,
> The fly shall marry a bumble bee.

Ask the children to tell you the two words that rhyme. (dee and bee)

Next, have the children listen to the whole rhyme.

> Fiddle-de-dee, fiddle-de-dee,
> The fly shall marry a bumble bee.
> They went to the church, and married was she:
> The fly had married the bumble-bee. (Mother Goose)

Ask the children for two rhyming words other than dee and bee. (she and bee)

AUDITORY DISCRIMINATION

SKILL: Discriminate the beginning sound of /f/

MATERIALS: None

Repeat the first pair of words below. Cover your mouth as the two words are pronounced. Have the students say "yes" if the words are the same, and "no" if they are not. Continue with remaining pairs.

fish and dish
fin and bin

fun and fun
fat and fit
fan and fan

INITIAL SOUND

ACTIVITY 1

SKILL: Discriminate beginning sound of /f/

MATERIALS: Felicia Fish worksheet 8.2

Introduce the Felicia Fish story. Read the story and ask the children to follow while listening for the words that begin with the /f/ phoneme. Read each sentence from the list below, and ask the children to say the words that begin with /f/.

1. Felicia Fish likes to swim. (Felicia, Fish)
2. Felicia Fish likes to swim with her family. (Felicia, Fish, family)
3. They play fast tag. (fast)
4. They tag each other on the fins. (fins)

ACTIVITY 2

SKILL: Identify /f/ beginning sounds in pictures and words

MATERIALS: Felicia Fish worksheets 8.1, 8.2, 8.3; magazines; scissors; glue; crayons; paper

Read the Felicia Fish story again, and ask the following questions:

1. What is the name of the fish in the story?
2. Name some other things that begin with the /f/ sound. (worksheet 8.3)
3. Hand out magazines and other materials. Have the students cut out /f/ beginning sound pictures and glue them on a separate sheet of paper.

BLENDING

SKILL: Blend sounds together to make a word

MATERIALS: None

The following are /f/ words. The words are divided into two parts: the /f/ sound and the rest of the word. Pronounce each word to the children one part at a time (repeat three times for each word), and ask them to guess the word.

f-ish	f-an	F-elicia
f-in	f-at	f-ast
f-amily		

SEGMENTATION

SKILL: Segment words into syllables

MATERIALS: The Felicia Fish story (worksheet 8.2)

Say /f/ words from the story and ask the children to clap one time for each word part.

Felicia - 3 claps	Fish - 1 clap
Family - 3 claps	Fast - 1 clap
Fins - 1 clap	

HOME ACTIVITY

SKILL: Identify the /f/ sound

MATERIALS: Worksheet 8.4, crayons, pencil

Parent instructs the child:

1. Take your pencil and trace the outline of Felicia Fish.
2. Color the picture of Felicia Fish.
3. What is this picture that begins with the /f/ sound?

/f/ as in Fish **67**

Felicia Fish

WORKSHEET 8.1

FELICIA FISH

Felicia Fish likes to swim. Felicia Fish likes to swim with her family. They play fast tag. They tag each other on the fins.

WORKSHEET 8.2

/f/ as in Fish 69

WORKSHEET 8.3

70 *Listening for Literacy*

Felicia Fish

WORKSHEET 8.4

CHAPTER 9

/s/ as in SEAL

SOUND PRODUCTION

ACTIVITY 1

SKILL: Produce phoneme /s/ sound

MATERIALS: Mirror

The /s/ phoneme is voiceless and classified as a fricative. The sound is produced by a stream of air emitted through a narrow opening between the teeth.

Have the children explore the shape of their mouths and placement of their lips as they make the /s/ sound. Give each child a small hand mirror to observe the production of the sound. The /s/ makes the snake sound.

ACTIVITY 2

SKILL: Repeat words beginning and ending with /s/ sound

MATERIALS: None

Model whole words that begin and end in the /s/ sound, and have the children repeat them.

Words that begin with /s/ include:

| sink | sock | Sam |
| sun | sat | seal |

Words that end with /s/ include:

ice	juice	house
boss	bus	toss

RHYMING

SKILL: Name two words that rhyme

MATERIALS: None

Share the following rhyme with the students. Have them listen very carefully and repeat back to you the first four lines.

> Sing a song of sixpence,
> A pocket full of rye;
> Four and twenty blackbirds
> Baked in a pie. (Mother Goose)

Ask the children to tell you the two words that rhyme. (rye and pie)

Next, have the children listen to the whole rhyme.

> Sing a song of sixpence,
> A pocket full of rye;
> Four and twenty blackbirds
> Baked in a pie.
>
> When the pie was opened,
> The birds began to sing;
> Was not that a dainty dish
> To set before the king. (Mother Goose)

Ask the children for two rhyming words other than rye and pie. (sing and king)

AUDITORY DISCRIMINATION

SKILL: Discriminate the beginning sound of /s/

MATERIALS: None

Repeat the first pair of words below. Cover your mouth as the two words are pronounced. Have the students say "yes" if the words are the same, and "no" if they are not. Continue with remaining pairs.

sea and tea
sock and sock
Sam and Pam
song and song
set and let

INITIAL SOUND

ACTIVITY 1

SKILL: Discriminate beginning sound of /s/

MATERIALS: Sammy Seal worksheet 9.2

Introduce the Sammy Seal story. Read the story and ask the children to follow while listening for the words that begin with the /s/ phoneme. Read each sentence from the list below, and ask the children to say the words that begin with /s/.

1. Sammy Seal likes to seesaw with his friend Suzie. (Sammy, Seal, seesaw, Suzie)
2. They sit on the seesaw as it goes up and down. (sit, seesaw)
3. Sammy Seal and Suzie also play in the sand. (Sammy, Seal, Suzie, sand)
4. The seals play in the park on Saturday. (seals, Saturday)

ACTIVITY 2

SKILL: Identify /s/ beginning sound in pictures and words

MATERIALS: Sammy Seal worksheets 9.1, 9.2, 9.3; magazines; scissors; glue; crayons; paper

Read the Sammy Seal story again, and ask the following questions:

1. What is the name of the seal in the story?
2. Name some other things that begin with the /s/ sound. (worksheet 9.3)
3. Hand out magazines and other materials. Have the students cut out /s/ beginning sound pictures and glue them on a separate sheet of paper.

BLENDING

SKILL: Blend sounds together to make a word

MATERIALS: None

The following are /s/ words. The words are divided into two parts: the /s/ sound and the rest of the word. Pronounce each word to the children one part at a time (repeat three times for each word), and ask them to guess the word.

| S-ammy | S-aturday | s-ock |
| s-eal | s-ea | s-eesaw |

SEGMENTATION

SKILL: Segment words into syllables

MATERIALS: The Sammy Seal story (worksheet 9.2)

Say the /s/ words from the story and ask the children to clap one time for each word part.

Sammy - 2 claps	Saturday - 3 claps
Seal - 1 clap	Sit - 1 clap
Suzie - 2 claps	Sand - 1 clap

HOME ACTIVITY

SKILL: Identify the /s/ sound

MATERIALS: Worksheet 9.4, crayons, pencil

Parent instructs the child:

1. Take your pencil and trace the outline of Sammy Seal.
2. Color the picture of Sammy Seal.
3. What is this picture that begins with the /s/ sound?

/s/ as in Seal

Sammy Seal

WORKSHEET 9.1

SAMMY SEAL

Sammy Seal likes to seesaw with his friend Suzie. They sit on the seesaw as it goes up and down. Sammy Seal and Suzie also play in the sand. The seals play in the park on Saturday.

/s/ as in Seal 77

WORKSHEET 9.3

78 *Listening for Literacy*

Sammy Seal

WORKSHEET 9.4

CHAPTER 10

/z/ as in ZEBRA

SOUND PRODUCTION

ACTIVITY 1

SKILL: Produce phoneme /z/ sound

MATERIALS: Mirror

The /z/ sound is voiced and classified as a fricative. The sound is produced by a stream of air emitted through a narrow opening between the teeth with phonation/voice.

Have the children explore the shape of their mouths and placement of their lips as they make the /z/ sound. Have them feel their vocal folds for the phonation. Give each child a small hand mirror to observe the production of the sound. The /z/ makes the buzzing bee sound.

ACTIVITY 2

SKILL: Repeat words beginning and ending with /z/ sound

MATERIALS: None

Model whole words that begin and end in the /z/ sound, and have the children repeat them.

Words that begin with /z/ include:

zoo	zipper	zoom
zip	zap	zero

Words that end with /z/ include:

buzz	fizz	whiz
size	jazz	fuzz

Many words that end with /s/ also sound like the /z/ phoneme, such as:

was	dues	nose
has	his	

RHYMING

SKILL: Name two words that rhyme

MATERIALS: None

Share the following rhyme with the students. Have them listen very carefully and repeat back to you the first two lines.

> Zip, zap, boom
> Zip, zap, zoom.

Ask the children to tell you the two words that rhyme. (zoom and boom)

Next, have the children listen to the whole rhyme.

> Zip, zap, boom
> Zip, zap, zoom.
> Zip, zap, groom
> Zip, zap, broom.

Ask the children for two rhyming words other than zoom and boom. (groom and broom)

AUDITORY DISCRIMINATION

SKILL: Discriminate the beginning sound of /z/

MATERIALS: None

Repeat the first pair of words below. Cover your mouth as the two words are pronounced. Have the students say "yes"

if the words are the same, and "no" if they are not. Continue with the remaining pairs.

> zoom and zoom
> zoo and boo
> zap and tap
> zip and dip
> zoo and zoo

INITIAL SOUND

ACTIVITY 1

SKILL: Discriminate beginning sound of /z/

MATERIALS: Zachary Zebra worksheet 10.2

Introduce the Zachary Zebra story. Read the story and ask the children to follow while listening for the words that begin with the /z/ phoneme. Read each sentence from the list below, and ask the children to say the words that begin with /z/.

1. Zachary Zebra lives in the zoo. (Zachary, Zebra, zoo)
2. A lot of animals live in the zoo with Zachary. (zoo, Zachary)
3. They like the zoo. (zoo)
4. Have you seen a zebra in the zoo? (zebra, zoo)

ACTIVITY 2

SKILL: Identify /z/ beginning sounds in pictures and words

MATERIALS: Zachary Zebra worksheets 10.1, 10.2, 10.3; magazines; scissors; glue; crayons; paper

Ask the students to remember the Zachary Zebra story, and ask the following questions.

1. What is the name of the zebra in the story?
2. Name some other things that begin with the /z/ sound. (worksheet 10.3)
3. Hand out magazines and other materials. Have the students cut out /z/ beginning sound pictures and glue them on a separate sheet of paper.

BLENDING

SKILL: Blend sounds together to make a word

MATERIALS: None

The following are /z/ words. The words are divided into two parts: the /z/ sound and the rest of the word. Pronounce each word to the children one part at a time (repeat three times for each word), and ask them to guess the word.

Z-achary	z-ip	z-ero
z-ebra	z-oo	z-one

SEGMENTATION

SKILL: Segment words into syllables

MATERIALS: The Zachary Zebra story (worksheet 10.2)

Say /z/ words from the story and ask the children to clap one time for each word part.

Zachary - 3 claps   Zebra - 2 claps
Zoo - 1 clap

HOME ACTIVITY

SKILL: Identify the /z/ sound

MATERIALS: Worksheet 10.4, crayons, pencil

Parent instructs the child:

1. Take your pencil and trace the outline of Zachary Zebra.
2. Color the picture of Zachary Zebra.
3. What is this picture that begins with the /z/ sound?

/z/ as in Zebra **83**

Zachary Zebra

WORKSHEET 10.1

ZACHARY ZEBRA

Zachary Zebra lives in the zoo. A lot of animals live in the zoo with Zachary. They like the zoo. Have you seen a zebra in the zoo?

/z/ as in Zebra   **85**

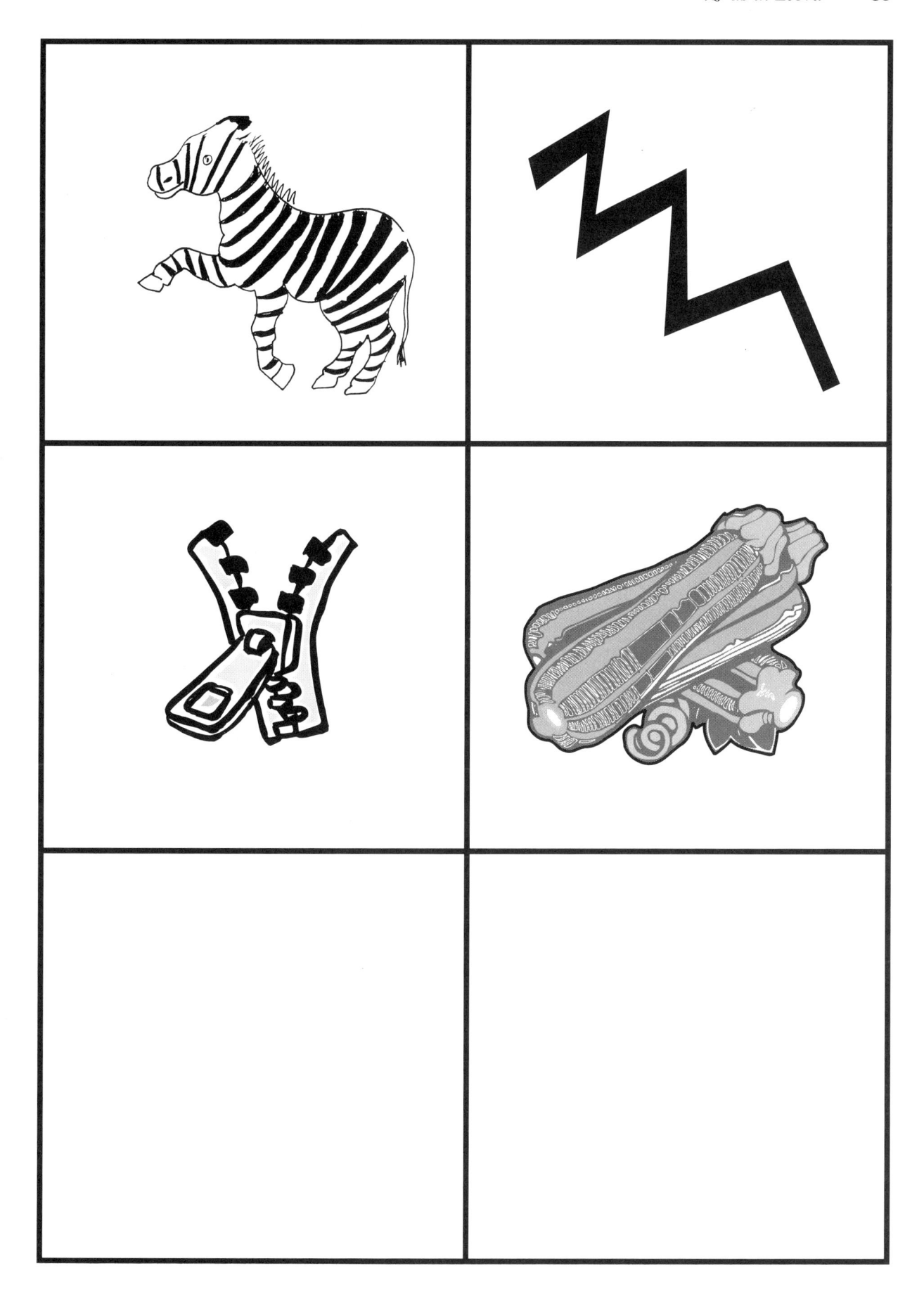

WORKSHEET 10.3

Zachary Zebra

WORKSHEET 10.4

/v/ as in VIXEN

CHAPTER 11

SOUND PRODUCTION

ACTIVITY 1

SKILL: Produce phoneme /v/ sound

MATERIALS: Mirror

The /v/ sound is frictive and is produced by placing the upper teeth on the lower lip and turning on the motor.

Have the children explore the shape of their mouths and placement of their lips as they make the /v/ sound. Have them feel their vocal folds for the phonation. Give each child a small hand mirror to observe the production of the sound. The /v/ makes the racing car sound.

ACTIVITY 2

SKILL: Repeat words beginning and ending with /v/ sound

MATERIALS: None

Model whole words that begin and end in the /v/ sound, and have the children repeat them.

Words that begin with /v/ include:

vote	vixen	vest
Vicky	van	

Words that end with /v/ include:

five   dove
love   hive

RHYMING

SKILL: Name two words that rhyme

MATERIALS: None

Share the following rhyme with the students. Have them listen very carefully and repeat back to you the first two lines.

>Vroom, Vroom goes the vacuum
>Picking up dirt all over the room.

Ask the children to tell you the two words that rhyme. (vroom and room)

Next, have the children listen to the whole rhyme.

>Vroom, vroom goes the vacuum
>Picking up dirt all over the room.
>Very, very quickly it runs
>Oh, vacuuming is such fun. (Authors)

Ask the children for two rhyming words other than vroom and room. (runs and fun)

AUDITORY DISCRIMINATION

SKILL: Discriminate the beginning sound of /v/

MATERIALS: None

Repeat the first pair of words below. Cover your mouth as the two words are pronounced. Have the students say "yes" if the words are the same, and "no" if they are not. Continue with the remaining pairs.

>van and van
>Vicky and Micky

vase and maze
vest and vest
vote and goat

INITIAL SOUND

ACTIVITY 1

SKILL: Discriminate beginning sound of /v/

MATERIALS: Vicky Vixen worksheet 11.2

Introduce the Vicky Vixen story. Read the story and ask the children to follow while listening for the words that begin with the /v/ phoneme. Read each sentence from the list below, and ask the children to say the words that begin with /v/.

1. Vicky Vixen is a fox with a brother named Vincent. (Vicky, Vixen, Vincent)
2. Vicky and Vincent live in a den in the valley. (Vicky, Vincent, valley)
3. Vicky is very sad because Vincent lost his voice. (Vicky, very, Vincent, voice)
4. The van will take him to th hospital to get a new voice. (van, voice)

ACTIVITY 2

SKILL: Identify /v/ beginning sound in pictures and words

MATERIALS: Vicky Vixen worksheets 11.1, 11.2, 11.3; magazines; scissors; glue; crayons; paper

Read the Vicky Vixen story again, and ask the following questions:

1. What is the name of the fox in the story?
2. Name some other things that begin with the /v/ sound. (worksheet 11.3)
3. Hand out magazines and other materials. Have the students cut out /v/ beginning sound pictures and glue them on a separate sheet of paper.

BLENDING

SKILL: Blend sounds together to make a word

MATERIALS: None

The following are /v/ words. The words are divided into two parts: the /v/ sound and the rest of the word. Pronounce each word to the children one part at a time (repeat three times for each word), and ask them to guess the word.

V-icky	v-ote	v-oice
v-ixen	v-an	v-alley
V-incent		

SEGMENTATION

SKILL: Segment words into syllables

MATERIALS: The Vicky Vixen story (worksheet 11.2)

Say /v/ words from the story and ask the children to clap one time for each word part.

Vicky - 2 claps	Vixen - 2 claps
Valley - 2 claps	Very - 2 claps
Voice - 1 clap	Van - 1 clap

HOME ACTIVITY

SKILL: Identify the /v/ sound

MATERIALS: Worksheet 11.4, crayons, pencil

Parent instructs the child:

1. Take your pencil and trace the outline of Vicky Vixen.
2. Color the picture of Vicky Vixen.
3. What is this picture that begins with the /v/ sound?

/v/ as in Vixen **91**

Vicky Vixen

WORKSHEET 11.1

VICKY VIXEN

Vicky Vixen is a fox with a brother named Vincent. Vicky and Vincent live in a den in the valley. Vicky is very sad because Vincent lost his voice. The van will take him to the hospital to get a new voice.

/v/ as in Vixen **93**

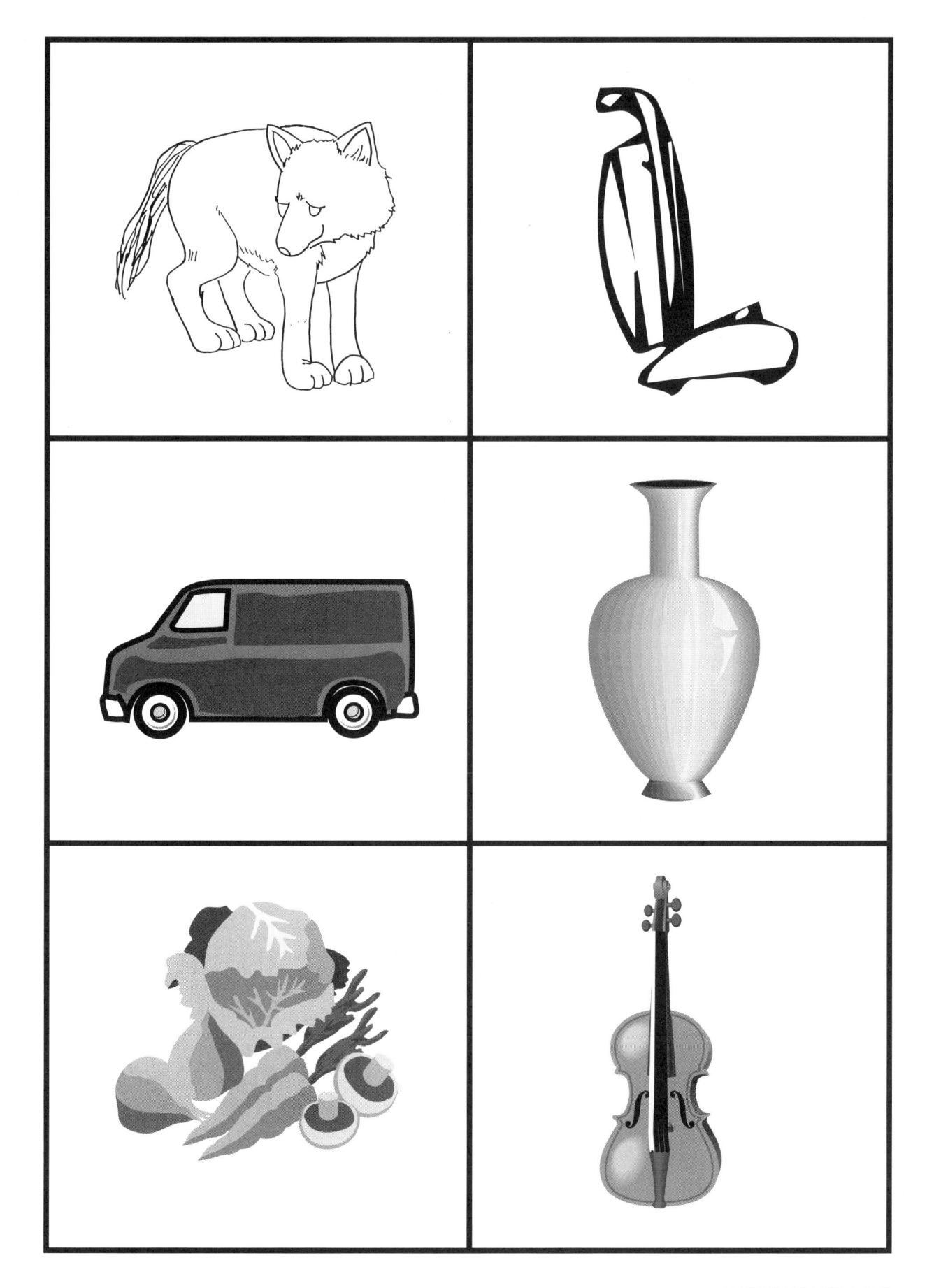

WORKSHEET 11.3

94　*Listening for Literacy*

Vicky Vixen

WORKSHEET 11.4

CHAPTER 12

/th/ as in THUMPY

SOUND PRODUCTION

ACTIVITY 1

SKILL: Produce phoneme /th/ sound

MATERIALS: Mirror

The /th/ sound is produced when the tongue is placed between the teeth and an air stream is emitted. Phonation only occurs with the voiced /th/. For the voiced /th/, there are a limited number of words and they carry little meaning.

Have the children explore the shape of their mouths as they make the /th/ sound. Give each child a small hand mirror to observe the production of the sound. The /th/ is the thump sound.

ACTIVITY 2

SKILL: Repeat words beginning and ending with /th/ sound

MATERIALS: None

Model whole words that begin and end in the /th/ sound, and have the children repeat them.

Unvoiced words that begin with /th/ include:

thump	thaw
thread	think

Unvoiced words that end with /th/ include:

path	math	breathe
bath	both	

Voiced words that begin with /th/ include:

this	these	them
that	those	the

RHYMING

SKILL: Name two words that rhyme

MATERIALS: None

Share the following rhyme with the students. Have them listen very carefully and repeat back to you the first two lines.

> Three little kittens
> Have lost their mittens
> And they began to cry.

Ask the children to tell you the two words that rhyme. (kittens and mittens)

Next, have the children listen to the whole rhyme.

> Three little kittens
> Have lost their mittens
> And they began to cry.
> Oh, Mother dear, our mittens we have lost.
> What? Lost your mittens.
> You naughty kittens.
> Then you shall have no pie. (Mother Goose)

Ask the children for two rhyming words other than kittens and mittens. (cry and pie)

AUDITORY DISCRIMINATION

SKILL: Discriminate the beginning sound of /th/

MATERIALS: None

Repeat the first pair of words below. Cover your mouth as the two words are pronounced. Have the students say "yes"

/th/ as in Thumpy   97

if the words are the same, and "no" if they are not. Continue with the remaining pairs.

>   think and sink
>   thump and thump
>   thicket and brisket
>   thick and thick
>   thimble and symbol

INITIAL SOUND

ACTIVITY 1

SKILL: Discriminate beginning sound of /th/

MATERIALS: Thumpy the Rabbit worksheet 12.2

Introduce the Thumpy the Rabbit story. Read the story and ask the children to follow while listening for the words that begin with the /th/ phoneme. Read each sentence from the list below, and ask the children to say the words that contain the /th/ sound.

1. Thumpy the rabbit thinks he will hop in the thicket. (Thumpy, the, thinks, the, thicket)
2. He is afraid that he will be scratched by the thorns. (that, the, thorns)
3. His fur is so thick that the thorns do not hurt. (thick, that, the, thorns)
4. He is so thankful that he hops up and down three times. (thankful, that, three)

ACTIVITY 2

SKILL: Identify /th/ beginning sounds in pictures and words

MATERIALS: Thumpy the Rabbit worksheets 12.1, 12.2, 12.3; magazines; scissors; glue; crayons; paper

Read the Thumpy the Rabbit story again, and ask the following questions:

1. What is the name of the rabbit in the story?
2. Name some other things that begin with the /th/ sound. (worksheet 12.3)

3. Hand out magazines and other materials. Have the students cut out /th/ beginning sound pictures and glue them on a separate sheet of paper.

BLENDING

SKILL: Blend sounds together to make a word

MATERIALS: None

The following are /th/ words. The words are divided into two parts: the /th/ sound and the rest of the word. Pronounce each word to the children one part at a time (repeat three times for each word), and ask them to guess the word.

th-icket	th-ump	th-ick
th-ink	th-umb	th-imble
th-ankful		

SEGMENTATION

SKILL: Segment words into syllables

MATERIALS: The Thumpy the Rabbit story (worksheet 12.2)

Say /th/ words from the story and ask the children to clap one time for each word part.

Thicket - 2 claps	Thorns - 1 clap
Thinks - 1 clap	Thankful - 2 claps
Thumpy - 2 claps	

HOME ACTIVITY

SKILL: Identify the /th/ sound

MATERIALS: Worksheet 12.4, crayons, pencil

Parent instructs the child:

1. Take your pencil and trace the outline of Thumpy the Rabbit.
2. Color the picture of Thumpy the Rabbit.
3. What is this picture that begins with the /th/ sound?

/th/ *as in Thumpy* **99**

WORKSHEET 12.1

THUMPY the RABBIT

Thumpy the rabbit thinks he will hop in the thicket. He is afraid that he will be scratched by the thorns. His fur is so thick that the thorns do not hurt. He is so thankful that he hops up and down three times.

WORKSHEET 12.2

/th/ as in Thumpy **101**

WORKSHEET 12.3

102 *Listening for Literacy*

WORKSHEET 12.4

CHAPTER 13

/sh/ as in SHEEP

SOUND PRODUCTION

ACTIVITY 1

SKILL: Produce phoneme /sh/ sound

MATERIALS: Mirror

The /sh/ sound is produced when a stream of air is emitted through a narrow opening. The tip of the tongue is elevated, and the lips are protruded and rounded. It is an unvoiced sound.

Have the children explore the shape of their mouths and placement of their lips as they make the /sh/ sound. Have them feel the air stream that is emitted. Give each child a small hand mirror to observe the production of the sound. The /sh/ sound is sometimes called the quiet sound.

ACTIVITY 2

SKILL: Repeat words beginning and ending with /sh/ sound

MATERIALS: None

Model whole words that begin and end in the /sh/ sound, and have the children repeat them.

Words that begin with /sh/ include:

shoe	she	shade
ship	shop	shake
sheep		

Words that end with /sh/ include:

dash	mash	fish
leash	wish	trash

RHYMING

SKILL: Name two words that rhyme

MATERIALS: None

Share the following rhyme with the students. Have them listen very carefully and repeat back to you the first four lines.

> There was an old woman
> Who lived in a shoe;
> She had so many children
> She didn't know what to do.

Ask the children to tell you the two words that rhyme. (shoe and do)

Next, have the children listen to the whole rhyme.

> There was an old woman
> Who lived in a shoe;
> She had so many children
> She didn't know what to do.
>
> She gave them some broth
> Without any bread;
> She whipped them all soundly,
> And put them to bed. (Mother Goose)

Ask the children for two rhyming words other than shoe and do. (bread and bed)

Another rhyme:

> Ba ba black sheep
> Have you any wool?
> Yes, sir, yes, sir
> Three bags full. (Mother Goose)

AUDITORY DISCRIMINATION

SKILL: Discriminate the beginning sound of /sh/

MATERIALS: None

Repeat two words with different beginning sounds. Cover the mouth as the two words are pronounced. Have the students say "yes" if the words are the same, and "no" if they are not.

> ship and rip
> sheep and sheep
> do and shoe
> shaggy and raggy
> shoe and shoe

INITIAL SOUND

ACTIVITY 1

SKILL: Discriminate beginning sound of /sh/

MATERIALS: Shoppy Sheep worksheet 13.2

Introduce the Shoppy Sheep story. Read the story and ask the children to follow while listening for the words that begin with the /sh/ phoneme. Read each sentence from the list below, and ask the children to say the words that begin with /sh/.

1. Shoppy Sheep was sitting in the shade of the big shaky tree. (Shoppy, Sheep, shade, shaky)
2. Along came a shaggy dog. (shaggy)
3. The shaggy dog barked at Shoppy Sheep and Shoppy Sheep was afraid. (shaggy, Shoppy, Sheep)
4. He ran away as fast as he could and hid in the shed. (shed)

ACTIVITY 2

SKILL: Identify /sh/ beginning sound in pictures and words

MATERIALS: Shoppy Sheep worksheets 13.1, 13.2, 13.3; magazines; scissors; glue; crayons; paper

Read the Shoppy Sheep story again, and ask the following questions:

1. What is the name of the sheep in the story?
2. Name some other things that begin with the /sh/ sound. (worksheet 13.3)
3. Hand out magazines and other materials. Have the students cut out /sh/ beginning sound pictures and glue them on a separate sheet of paper.

BLENDING

SKILL: Blend sounds together to make a word

MATERIALS: None

The following are /sh/ words. The words are divided into two parts: the /sh/ sound and the rest of the word. Pronounce each word to the children one part at a time (repeat three times for each word), and ask them to guess the word.

    sh-oppy   sh-ade
    sh-eep   sh-aggy

SEGMENTATION

SKILL: Segment words into syllables

MATERIALS: The Shoppy Sheep story (worksheet 13.2)

Say the /sh/ words from the story and ask the children to clap one time for each word part.

    Shoppy - 2 claps   Sheep - 1 clap
    Shade - 1 clap   Shaggy - 2 claps

HOME ACTIVITY

SKILL: Identify the /sh/ sound

MATERIALS: Worksheet 13.4, crayons, pencil

Parent instructs the child:

1. Take your pencil and trace the outline of Shoppy Sheep.
2. Color the picture of Shoppy Sheep.
3. What is this picture that begins with the /sh/ sound?

/sh/ as in Sheep **107**

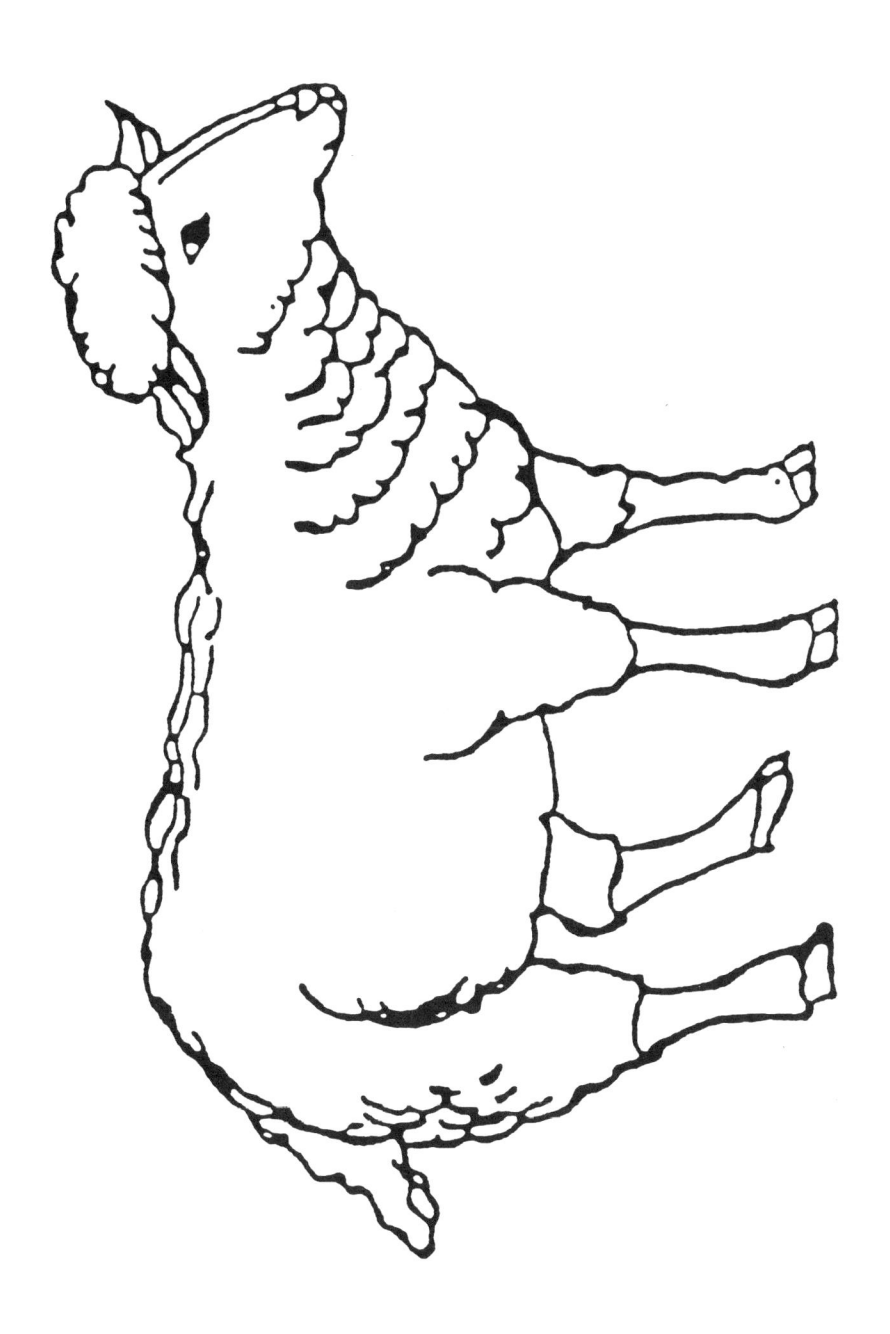

Shoppy Sheep

WORKSHEET 13.1

SHOPPY SHEEP

Shoppy **Sh**eep was sitting in the **sh**ade of the big **sh**aky tree. Along came a **sh**aggy dog. The **sh**aggy dog barked at **Sh**oppy **Sh**eep and **Sh**oppy **Sh**eep was afraid. He ran away as fast as he could and hid in the **sh**ed.

/sh/ as in Sheep   **109**

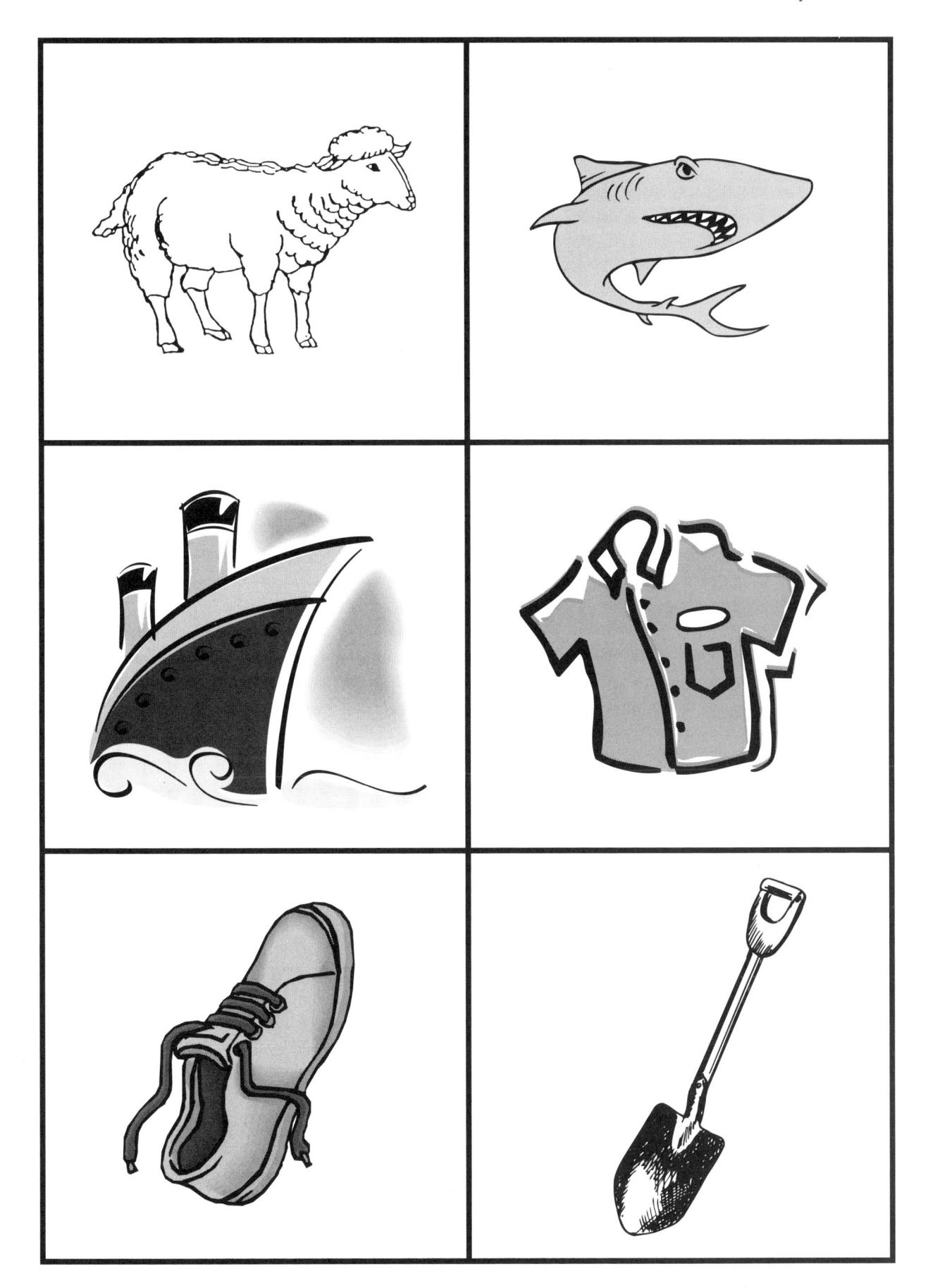

WORKSHEET 13.3

110 *Listening for Literacy*

Shoppy Sheep

WORKSHEET 13.4

CHAPTER 14

/ch/ as in CHICKEN

SOUND PRODUCTION

ACTIVITY 1

SKILL: Produce phoneme /ch/ sound

MATERIALS: Mirror

The /ch/ sound is a voiceless consonant. The tongue is placed on the ridge of the mouth behind the teeth and breath passes through. There is a complete closure of the vocal tract followed by a slow release of air.

Have the children explore the shape of their mouths and placement of their lips as they make the /ch/ sound. Give each child a small hand mirror to observe the production of the sound. The /ch/ sound is often called the "choo choo" sound.

ACTIVITY 2

SKILL: Repeat words beginning and ending with /ch/ sound

MATERIALS: None

Model whole words that begin and end in the /ch/ sound, and have the children repeat them.

Words that begin with /ch/ include:

choo choo	chain	chin
chew	chair	Charlie

Words that end with /ch/ include:

ouch	teach	witch
touch	lunch	match
itch		

RHYMING

SKILL: Name two words that rhyme

MATERIALS: None

Share the following rhyme with the students. Have them listen very carefully and repeat back to you the first two lines.

>   The children go clap, clap
>   Then they go tap, tap

Ask the children to tell you the two words that rhyme. (clap and tap)

Next, have the children listen to the whole rhyme.

>   The children go clap, clap
>   Then they go tap, tap
>   Next, they go nap, nap
>   After running a lap (Authors)

Ask the children for two rhyming words other than clap and tap. (nap and lap)

AUDITORY DISCRIMINATION

SKILL: Discriminate the beginning sound of /ch/

MATERIALS: None

Repeat the first pair of words below. Cover your mouth as the two words are pronounced. Have the students say "yes" if the words are the same, and "no" if they are not. Continue with the remaining pairs.

>   chin and chin
>   chick and thick

chop and chop
chew and mew
cheep and peep

INITIAL SOUND

ACTIVITY 1

SKILL: Discriminate beginning sound of /ch/

MATERIALS: Chicky Chicken worksheet 14.2

Introduce the Chicky Chicken story. Read the story and ask the children to follow while listening for the words that begin with the /ch/ phoneme. Read each sentence from the list below, and ask the children to say the words that begin with /ch/.

1. Chicky Chicken lives on the farm. (Chicky, chicken)
2. He likes to say cheep, cheep and chirp, chirp. (cheep, chirp)
3. He is a chatter box. (chatter)
4. He runs and hides when he plays with the children. (children)

ACTIVITY 2

SKILL: Identify /ch/ beginning sounds in pictures and words

MATERIALS: Chicky Chicken worksheets 14.1, 14.2, 14.3; magazines; scissors; glue; crayons; paper

Read the Chicky Chicken story again, and ask the following questions.

1. What is the name of the chicken in the story?
2. Name some other things that begin with the /ch/ sound. (worksheet 14.3)
3. Hand out magazines and other materials. Have the students cut out /ch/ beginning sound pictures and glue them on a separate sheet of paper.

BLENDING

SKILL: Blend sounds together to make a word

MATERIALS: None

The following are /ch/ initial sound words. The words are divided into two parts: the /ch/ sound and the rest of the word. Pronounce each word to the children one part at a time (repeat three times for each word), and ask them to guess the word.

ch-icky	ch-air	ch-oo
ch-eep	ch-icken	ch-in
ch-irp	ch-ildren	ch-atter

SEGMENTATION

SKILL: Segment words into syllables

MATERIALS: The Chicky Chicken story (worksheet 14.2)

Say /ch/ words from the story and ask the children to clap one time for each word part.

Chicky - 2 claps	Chicken - 2 claps
Cheep - 1 clap	Chirp - 1 clap
Chatter - 2 claps	Children - 2 claps

HOME ACTIVITY

SKILL: Identify the /ch/ sound

MATERIALS: Worksheet 14.4, crayons, pencil

Parent instructs the child:

1. Take your pencil and trace the outline of Chicky Chicken.
2. Color the picture of Chicky Chicken.
3. What is this picture that begins with the /ch/ sound?

/ch/ as in Chicken **115**

Chicky Chicken

WORKSHEET 14.1

CHICKY CHICKEN

Chicky **Ch**icken lives on the farm. He likes to say **ch**eep, **ch**eep and **ch**irp, **ch**irp. He is a **ch**atter box. He runs and hides when he plays with the **ch**ildren.

/ch/ as in Chicken 117

WORKSHEET 14.3

118 *Listening for Literacy*

Chicky chicken

WORKSHEET 14.4

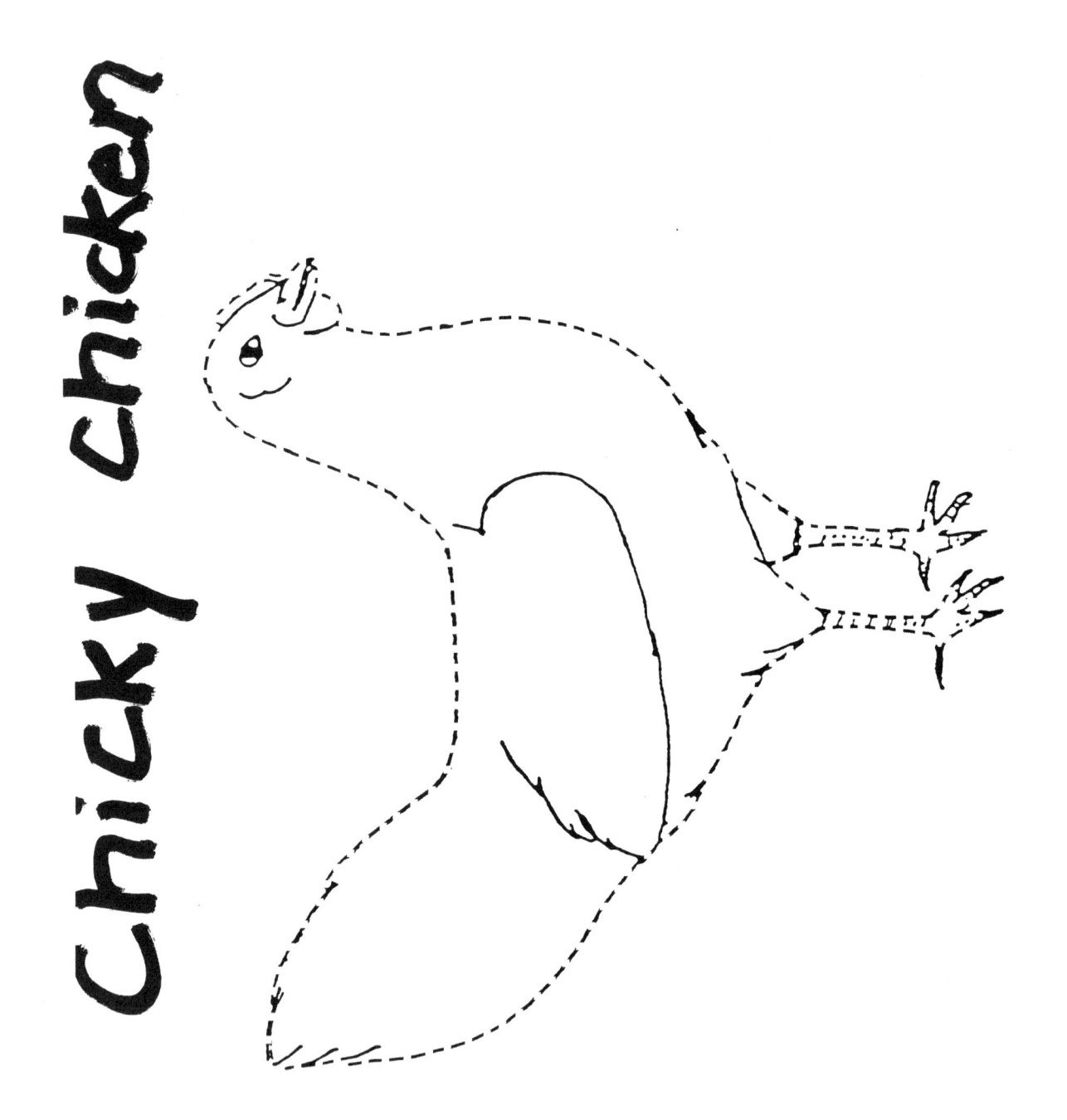

CHAPTER 15

/J/ as in JELLYFISH

SOUND PRODUCTION

ACTIVITY 1

SKILL: Produce phoneme /j/ sound

MATERIALS: Mirror

The /j/ sound is a voiced sound. Have the children explore the shape of their mouths and placement of their lips as they make the /j/ sound. Have them feel their vocal folds for the phonation. Give each child a small hand mirror to observe the production of the sound. The /j/ sound is the jumping sound.

ACTIVITY 2

SKILL: Repeat words beginning and ending with /j/ sound

MATERIALS: None

Model whole words that begin and end in the /j/ sound, and have the children repeat them.

Words that begin with /j/ include:

| juice | jump | George |
| joke | jelly | |

Words that end with /j/ include:

> edge
> bridge
> cabbage

RHYMING

SKILL: Name two words that rhyme

MATERIALS: None

Share the following rhyme with the students. Have them listen very carefully and repeat back to you the first three lines.

> Jack be nimble,
> And Jack be quick;
> And Jack jump over the candlestick. (Mother Goose)

Ask the children to tell you the two words that rhyme. (quick and candlestick)

AUDITORY DISCRIMINATION

SKILL: Discriminate the beginning sound of /j/

MATERIALS: None

Repeat the first pair of words below. Cover your mouth as the two words are pronounced. Have the students say "yes" if the words are the same, and "no" if they are not. Continue with the remaining pairs.

> Jack and Jack
> jump and bump
> jingle and dingle
> jet and bet
> joke and joke

INITIAL SOUND

ACTIVITY 1

SKILL: Discriminate beginning sound of /j/

MATERIALS: Jack Jellyfish worksheet 15.2

Introduce the Jack Jellyfish story. Read the story and ask the children to follow while listening for the words that begin with the /j/ phoneme. Read each sentence from the list below, and ask the children to say the words that begin with /j/.

1. Jack Jellyfish jumps rope and juggles. (Jack, Jellyfish, jumps, juggles)
2. Jack Jellyfish jumps with joy. (Jack, Jellyfish, jumps, joy)
3. Jack Jellyfish is jolly when he jumps and juggles. (Jack, Jellyfish, jolly, jumps, juggles)
4. He jumps and juggles in July. (jumps, juggles, July)

ACTIVITY 2

SKILL: Identify /j/ beginning sounds in pictures and words

MATERIALS: Jack Jellyfish worksheets 15.1, 15.2, 15.3; magazines; scissors; glue; crayons; paper

Read the Jack Jellyfish story again, and ask the following questions:

1. What is the name of the jellyfish in the story?
2. Name some other things that begin with the /j/ sound. (worksheet 15.3)
3. Hand out magazines and other materials. Have the students cut out /j/ beginning sound pictures and glue them on a separate sheet of paper.

BLENDING

SKILL: Blend sounds together to make a word

MATERIALS: None

The following are /j/ words. The words are divided into two parts: the /j/ sound and the rest of the word. Pronounce each word to the children one part at a time (repeat three times for each word), and ask them to guess the word.

J-ack	j-elly	j-uggles
j-ump	j-am	J-uly
j-olly		

SEGMENTATION

SKILL: Segment words into syllables

MATERIALS: The Jack Jellyfish story (worksheet 15.2)

Say /j/ words from the story and ask the children to clap one time for each word part.

Jack - 1 clap	Jellyfish - 3 claps
Jumps - 1 clap	Juggles - 2 claps
Jolly - 2 claps	July - 2 claps

HOME ACTIVITY

SKILL: Identify the /j/ sound

MATERIALS: Worksheet 15.4, crayons, pencil

Parent instructs the child:

1. Take your pencil and trace the outline of Jack Jellyfish.
2. Color the picture of Jack Jellyfish.
3. What is this picture that begins with the /j/ sound?

/J/ as in Jack **123**

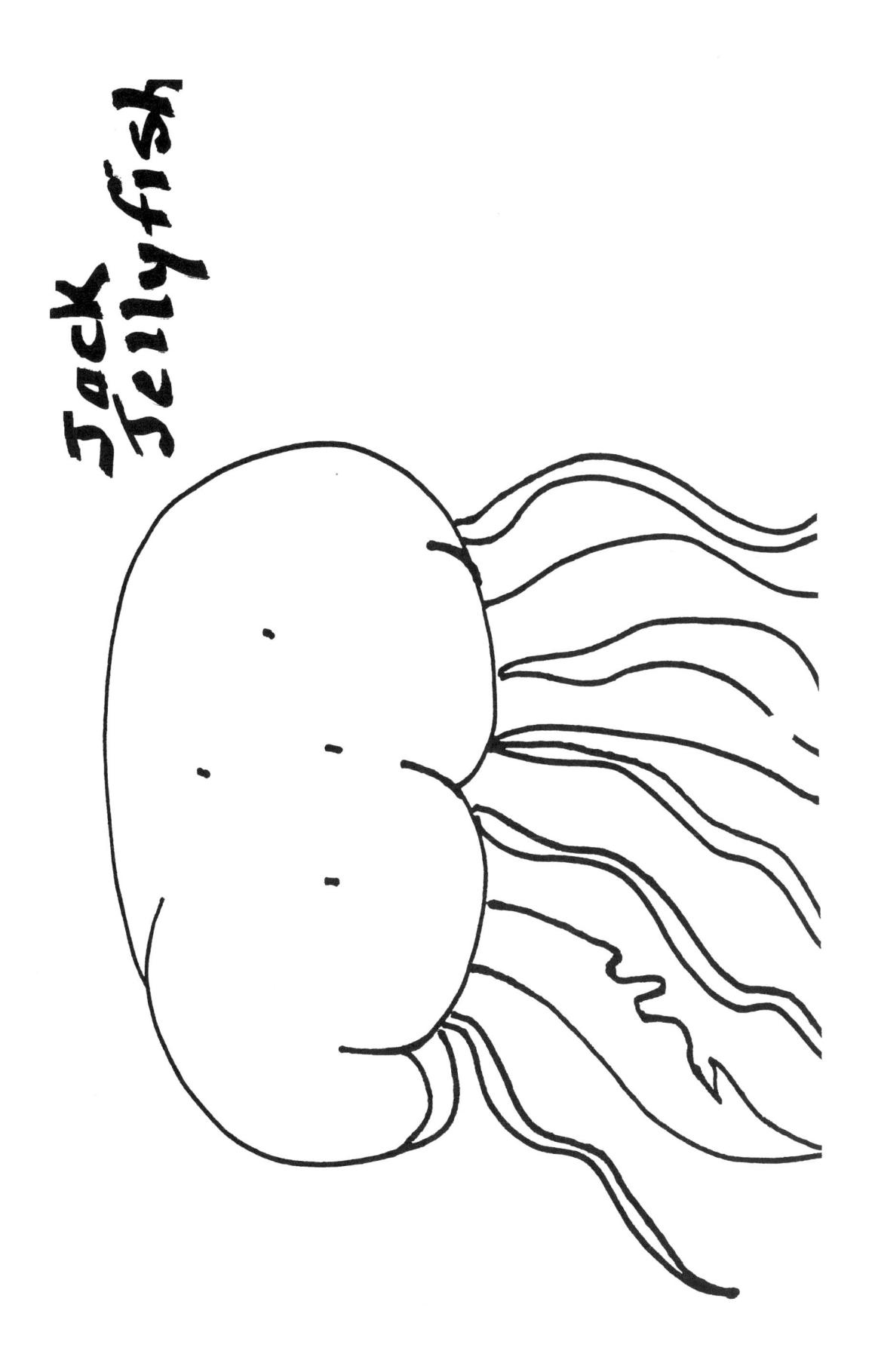

Jack Jellyfish

WORKSHEET 15.1

JACK JELLYFISH

Jack Jellyfish jumps rope and juggles. Jack Jellyfish jumps with joy. Jack Jellyfish is jolly when he jumps and juggles. He jumps and juggles in July.

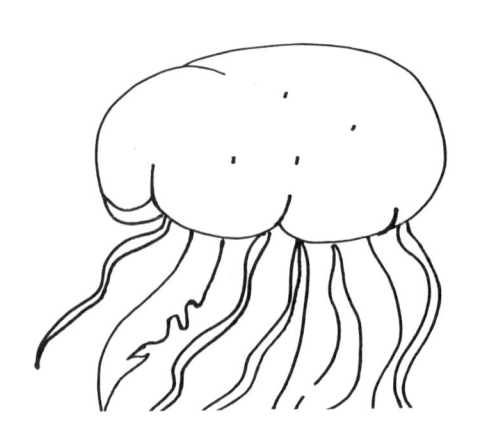

/J/ as in Jack   **125**

WORKSHEET 15.3

126 *Listening for Literacy*

Jack Jellyfish

WORKSHEET 15.4

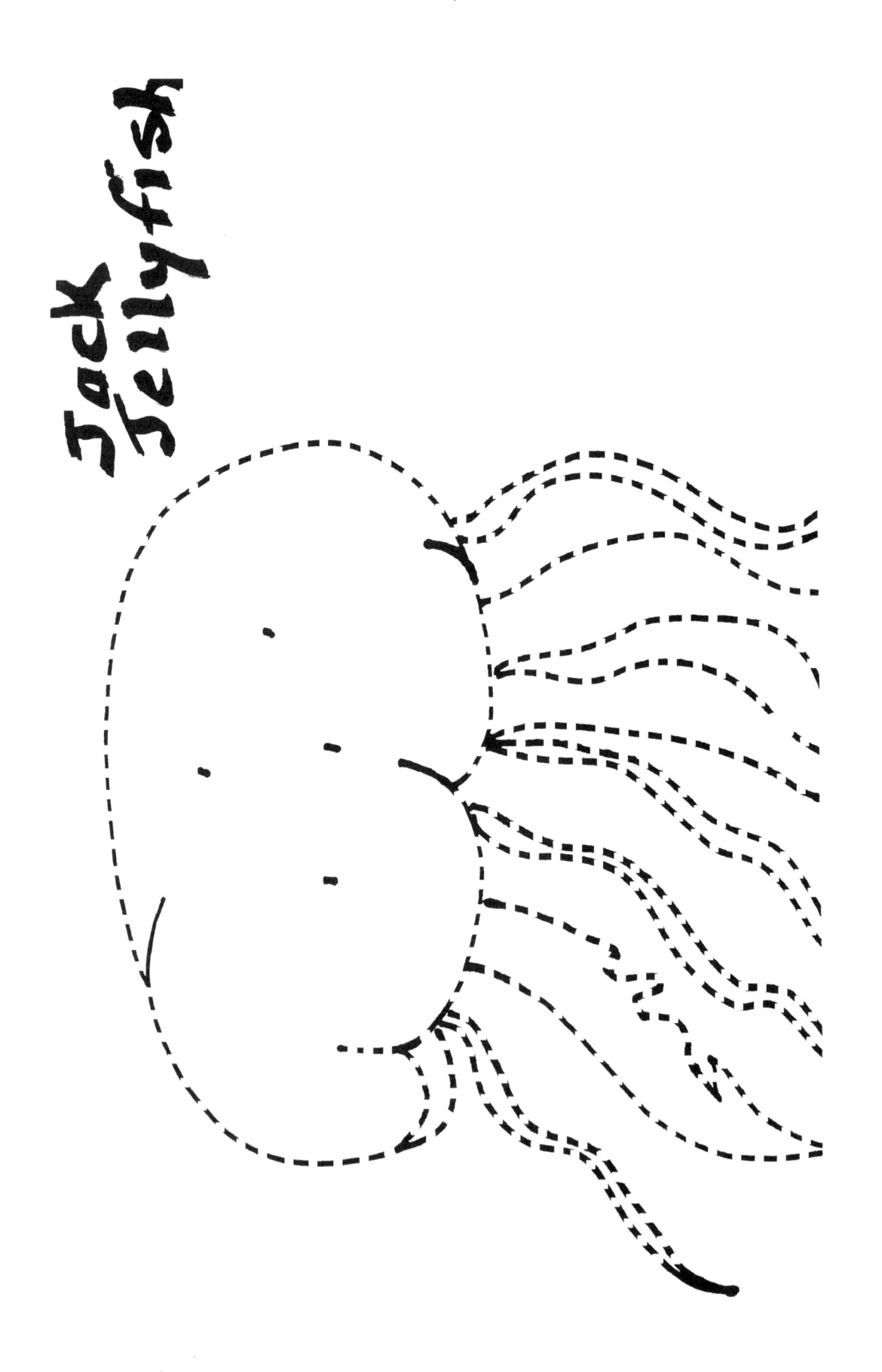

CHAPTER 16

/n/ as in NEWT

SOUND PRODUCTION

ACTIVITY 1

SKILL: Produce phoneme /n/ sound

MATERIALS: Mirror

The /n/ sound is voiced and nasal. It is one of the three nasal sounds in the English language (/m/, /n/, /ing/). The tongue is placed on the ridge behind the teeth, and vibrations are felt by touching the side of the nose with the fingertips.

Have the children explore the shape of their mouths as they make the /n/ sound. Instruct them to turn on their voice motors, lift the tip of their tongues, and make the air come through the nose. Give each child a small hand mirror to observe the production of the sound. The /n/ makes the neighing sound, like a horse.

ACTIVITY 2

SKILL: Repeat words beginning and ending with /n/ sound

MATERIALS: None

Model whole words that begin and end in the /n/ sound, and have the children repeat them.

127

Words that begin with /n/ include:

| nut | night | name |
| nice | nest | nickel |

Words that end with /n/ include:

open	rain	ran
ten	run	brown
train		

RHYMING

SKILL: Name two words that rhyme

MATERIALS: None

Share the following rhyme with the students. Have them listen very carefully and repeat back to you the first four lines.

> I had a little nut tree,
> Nothing would it bear.
> But a silver nutmeg
> And a golden pear. (Authors)

Ask the children to tell you the two words that rhyme. (bear and pear)

AUDITORY DISCRIMINATION

SKILL: Discriminate the beginning sound of /n/

MATERIALS: None

Repeat the first pair of words below. Cover your mouth as the two words are pronounced. Have the students say "yes" if the words are the same, and "no" if they are not. Continue with the remaining pairs.

nut and cut
name and name
nest and vest
nice and nice

INITIAL SOUND

ACTIVITY 1

SKILL: Discriminate beginning sound of /n/

MATERIALS: Nigel Newt worksheet 16.2

Introduce the Nigel Newt story. Read the story and ask the children to follow while listening for the words that begin with the /n/ phoneme. Read each sentence from the list below, and ask the children to say the words that begin with /n/.

1. Nigel Newt looks like a lizard and lives near water. (Nigel, Newt, near)
2. Nigel Newt has a nice friend named Ned. (Nigel, Newt, nice, named, Ned)
3. They eat nachos and nap at night. (nachos, nap, night)
4. Nigel Newt and Ned smell the night air with their noses. (Nigel, Newt, Ned, night, noses)

ACTIVITY 2

SKILL: Identify /n/ beginning sounds in pictures and words

MATERIALS: Nigel Newt worksheets 16.1, 16.2, 16.3; magazines; scissors; glue; crayons; paper

Read the Nigel Newt story again, and ask the following questions:

1. What is the name of the newt in the story?
2. Name some other things that begin with the /n/ sound. (worksheet 16.3)
3. Hand out magazines and other materials. Have the students cut out /n/ beginning sound pictures and glue them on a separate sheet of paper.

BLENDING

SKILL: Blend sounds together to make a word

MATERIALS: None

The following are /n/ words. The words are divided into two parts: the /n/ sound and the rest of the word. Pronounce each word to the children one part at a time (repeat three times for each word), and ask them to guess the word.

N-igel	n-ear	n-ut
n-ewt	n-ot	n-ail
n-ap	n-ight	n-achos

SEGMENTATION

SKILL: Segment words into syllables

MATERIALS: The Nigel Newt story (worksheet 16.2)

Say /n/ words from e story and ask the children to clap one time for each word part.

Nigel - 2 claps	Newt - 1 clap
Ned - 1 clap	Nachos - 2 claps
Night - 1 clap	Noses - 2 claps
Nap - 1 clap	

HOME ACTIVITY

SKILL: Identify the /n/ sound

MATERIALS: Worksheet 16.4, crayons, pencil

Parent instructs the child:

1. Take your pencil and trace the outline of Nigel Newt.
2. Color the picture of Nigel Newt.
3. What is this picture that begins with the /n/ sound?

/n/ as in Newt **131**

Nigel Newt

WORKSHEET 16.1

NIGEL NEWT

Nigel Newt looks like a lizard and lives near water. Nigel Newt has a friend named Ned. They eat nachos and nap at night. Nigel Newt and Ned smell the night air with their noses.

/n/ as in Newt   **133**

WORKSHEET 16.3

134   *Listening for Literacy*

Nigel Newt

WORKSHEET 16.4

/l/ as in LION

CHAPTER 17

SOUND PRODUCTION

ACTIVITY 1

SKILL: Produce phoneme /l/ sound

MATERIALS: Mirror

The /l/ sound is voiced. Sometimes it is classified as a semi vowel. The tip of the tongue is raised to the gum ridge behind the upper teeth. Slight pressure is applied. The breath stream flows freely around the two sides of the tongue.

Have the children explore the shape of their mouths as they make the /l/ sound. Have them feel their vocal folds for the phonation. Give each child a small hand mirror to observe the production of the sound. This sound is the singing sound (la, la, la).

ACTIVITY 2

SKILL: Repeat words beginning and ending with /l/ sound

MATERIALS: None

Model whole words that begin and end in the /l/ sound, and have the children repeat them.

Words that begin with /l/ include:

| late | lady | like |
| little | leg | |

Words that end with /l/ include:

nail	little	doll
full	gentle	turtle

RHYMING

SKILL: Name two words that rhyme

MATERIALS: None

Share the following rhyme with the students. Have them listen very carefully and repeat back to you the first four lines.

> Ladybug, ladybug,
> Fly away, do,
> Fly to the mountain,
> And feed upon dew.

Ask the children to tell you the two words that sound alike. (do and dew)

Next, have the children listen to the whole rhyme.

> Ladybug, ladybug
> Fly away, do,
> Fly to the mountain,
> And feed upon dew,
> Feed upon dew,
> And sleep on a rug,
> And then run away,
> Like a good little bug. (Mother Goose)

Ask the children for two rhyming words other than do and dew. (rug and bug)

AUDITORY DISCRIMINATION

SKILL: Discriminate the beginning sound of /l/

MATERIALS: None

Repeat the first pair of words below. Cover your mouth as the two words are pronounced. Have the students say "yes"

if the words are the same, and "no" if they are not. Continue with the remaining pairs.

> lick and kick
> little and little
> leg and leg
> light and night

INITIAL SOUND

ACTIVITY 1

SKILL: Discriminate beginning sound of /l/

MATERIALS: Larry Lion worksheet 17.2

Introduce the Larry Lion story. Read the story and ask the children to follow while listening for the words that begin with the /l/ phoneme. Read each sentence from the list below, and ask the children to say the words that begin with /l/.

1. Larry Lion lives at the zoo. (Larry, Lion, lives)
2. His yard has a large fence so he can't get loose. (large, loose)
3. Larry likes to watch people go by. (Larry, likes)
4. Larry loves to lick lollipops. (Larry, loves, lick, lollipops)

ACTIVITY 2

SKILL: Identify /l/ beginning sounds in pictures and words

MATERIALS: Larry Lion worksheets 17.1, 17.2, 17.3; magazines; scissors; glue; crayons; paper

Read the Larry Lion story again, and ask the following questions:

1. What is the name of the lion in the story?
2. Name some other things that begin with the /l/ sound. (worksheet 17.3)
3. Hand out magazines and other materials. Have the students cut out /l/ beginning sound pictures and glue them on a separate sheet of paper.

BLENDING

SKILL: Blend sounds together to make a word

MATERIALS: None

The following are /l/ words. The words are divided into two parts: the /l/ sound and the rest of the word. Pronounce each word to the children one part at a time (repeat three times for each word), and ask them to guess the word.

L-arry	l-oves	l-arge
l-ives	l-ion	l-oose
l-ick		

SEGMENTATION

SKILL: Segment words into syllables

MATERIALS: The Larry Lion story (worksheet 17.2)

Say /l/ words from the story and ask the children to clap one time for each word part.

Larry - 2 claps	Lion - 2 claps
Large - 1 clap	Loose - 1 clap
Lick - 1 clap	Lollipops - 3 claps

HOME ACTIVITY

SKILL: Identify the /l/ sound

MATERIALS: Worksheet 17.4, crayons, pencil

Parent instructs the child:

1. Take your pencil and trace the outline of Larry Lion.
2. Color the picture of Larry Lion.
3. What is this picture that begins with the /l/ sound?

/l/ as in Lion **139**

Larry Lion

WORKSHEET 17.1

LARRY LION

Larry Lion lives at the zoo. His yard has a large fence so he can't get loose. Larry likes to watch people go by. Larry loves to lick lollipops.

WORKSHEET 17.2

/l/ as in Lion   **141**

WORKSHEET 17.3

142 *Listening for Literacy*

WORKSHEET 17.4

CHAPTER 18

/r/ as in RABBIT

SOUND PRODUCTION

ACTIVITY 1

SKILL: Produce phoneme /r/ sound

MATERIALS: Mirror

The /r/ sound is voiced. It is considered a semi vowel and a glide. The sound is made by raising the middle portion of the tongue to the palate.

Have the children explore the shape of their mouths as they make the /r/ sound. Have them feel their vocal folds for the phonation. Give each child a small hand mirror to observe the production of the sound. The /r/ makes the motor sound or roaring sound.

ACTIVITY 2

SKILL: Repeat words beginning and ending with /r/ sound

MATERIALS: None

Model whole words that begin and end in the /r/ sound, and have the children repeat them.

Words that begin with /r/ include:

| rabbit | red | ran |
| read | rose | |

144 *Listening for Literacy*

Words that end with /r/ include:

    river   silver   teacher
    rider   stair

RHYMING

SKILL: Name two words that rhyme

MATERIALS: None

Share the following rhyme with the students. Have them listen very carefully and repeat back to you the first two lines.

    Rub a dub dub,
    Three men in a tub:

Ask the children to tell you the two words that rhyme. (dub and tub)

Next, have the children listen to the whole rhyme.

    Rub a dub dub,
    Three men in a tub:
    And who do you think they be?
    The butcher, the baker,
    The candlestick maker;
    Turn 'em out, knaves all three. (Mother Goose)

Ask the children for two rhyming words other than dub and rub. (be and three/maker and baker)

AUDITORY DISCRIMINATION

SKILL: Discriminate the beginning sound of /r/

MATERIALS: None

Repeat the first pair of words below. Cover your mouth as the two words are pronounced. Have the students say "yes" if the words are the same, and "no" if they are not. Continue with the remaining pairs.

    rock and dock
    rub and dub
    ring and ring

red and said
road and road

INITIAL SOUND

ACTIVITY 1

SKILL: Discriminate beginning sound of /r/

MATERIALS: Rachel Rabbit worksheet 18.2

Introduce the Rachel Rabbit story. Read the story and ask the children to follow while listening for the words that begin with the /r/ phoneme. Read each sentence from the list below, and ask the children to say the words that begin with /r/.

1. Rachel Rabbit rides her red bike. (Rachel, Rabbit, rides, red)
2. The wheels on the bike go round and round. (round)
3. When she sees her friend Ruthie she rings her bell. (Ruthie, rings)
4. Ruthie's bike goes rattle, rattle. (Ruthie, rattle)

ACTIVITY 2

SKILL: Identify /r/ beginning sounds in pictures and words

MATERIALS: Rachel Rabbit worksheets 18.1, 18.2, 18.3; magazines; scissors; glue; crayons; paper

Read the Rachel Rabbit story again, and ask the following questions:

1. What is the name of the rabbit in the story?
2. Name some other things that begin with the /r/ sound. (worksheet 18.3)
3. Hand out magazines and other materials. Have the students cut out /r/ beginning sound pictures and glue them on a separate sheet of paper.

BLENDING

SKILL: Blend sounds together to make a word

MATERIALS: None

The following are /r/ words. The words are divided into two parts: the /r/ sound and the rest of the word. Pronounce each word to the children one part at a time (repeat three times for each word), and ask them to guess the word.

R-achel	r-ides	r-ound
r-abbit	r-ed	r-ing

SEGMENTATION

SKILL: Segment words into syllables

MATERIALS: The Rachel Rabbit story (worksheet 18.2)

Say /r/ words from the story and ask the children to clap one time for each word part.

Rachel - 2 claps	Rabbit - 2 claps
Rides - 1 clap	Red - 1 clap
Round - 1 clap	Ruthie - 2 claps
Rings - 1 clap	Rattle - 2 claps

HOME ACTIVITY

SKILL: Identify the /r/ sound

MATERIALS: Worksheet 18.4, crayons, pencil

Parent instructs the child:

1. Take your pencil and trace the outline of Rachel Rabbit.
2. Color the picture of Rachel Rabbit.
3. What is this picture that begins with the /r/ sound?

/r/ as in Rabbit **147**

Rachel Rabbit

WORKSHEET 18.1

RACHEL RABBIT

Rachel **R**abbit **r**ides her **r**ed bike. The wheels on the bike go **r**ound and **r**ound. When she sees her friend **R**uthie, she **r**ings her bell. **R**uthie's bike goes **r**attle, **r**attle.

/r/ as in Rabbit **149**

WORKSHEET 18.3

150   *Listening for Literacy*

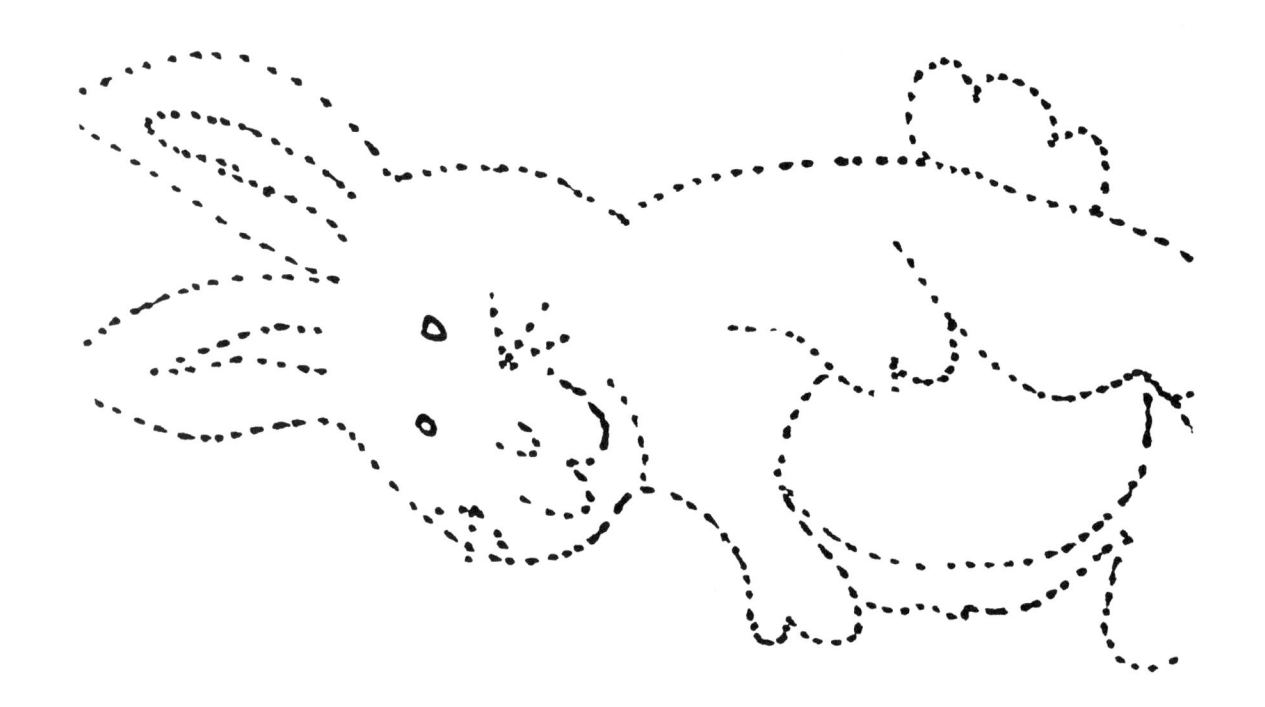

WORKSHEET 18.4

CHAPTER 19

/y/ as in YAK

SOUND PRODUCTION

ACTIVITY 1

SKILL: Produce phoneme /y/ sound

MATERIALS: Mirror

The /y/ sound is classified as a glide continuant and semi-vowel. A semivowel seems vowel-like or consonant-like depending on position in the articulatory sequence. A glide is so named because production requires movement of the articulators from one position to another. Production of a continuant requires a continuous stream of air.

Have the children explore the shape of their mouths as they make the /y/ sound. Have them feel their vocal folds for the phonation. Give each child a small hand mirror to observe the production of the sound. The /y/ sounds like a yipping puppy.

ACTIVITY 2

SKILL: Repeat words beginning with /y/ sound

MATERIALS: None

Model whole words that begin and end in the /y/ sound, and have the children repeat them.

Words that begin with /y/ include:

| yak | yet | year |
| yellow | yarn | yes |

RHYMING

SKILL: Name two words that rhyme

MATERIALS: None

Share the following rhyme with the students. Have them listen very carefully and repeat back to you the first two lines.

> Yackety, Yackety
> I'll come back
> and that's a fact. (Authors)

Ask the children to tell you the two words that rhyme. (back and fact)

AUDITORY DISCRIMINATION

SKILL: Discriminate the beginning sound of /y/

MATERIALS: None

Repeat the first pair of words below. Cover your mouth as the two words are pronounced. Have the students say "yes" if the words are the same, and "no" if they are not. Continue with the remaining pairs.

> yak and yak
> yellow and mellow
> yum and yum
> yarn and barn
> year and dear

INITIAL SOUND

ACTIVITY 1

SKILL: Discriminate beginning sound of /y/

MATERIALS: Yancy Yak worksheet 19.2

Introduce the Yancy Yak story. Read the story and ask the children to follow while listening for the words that begin with the /y/ phoneme. Read each sentence from the list below, and ask the children to say the words that begin with /y/.

1. Young Yancy Yak played in the yard yesterday. (Young, Yancy, Yak, yard, yesterday)
2. He played with a yucky, yellow ball of yarn. (yucky, yellow, yarn)
3. When he finished playing, Yancy ate something yummy. (Yancy, yummy)
4. It was yummy, yellow yogurt. (yummy, yellow, yogurt)

ACTIVITY 2

SKILL: Identify /y/ beginning sounds in pictures and words

MATERIALS: Yancy Yak worksheets 19.1, 19.2, 19.3; magazines; scissors; glue; crayons; paper

Read the Yancy Yak story again, and ask the following questions:

1. What is the name of the yak in the story?
2. Name some other things that begin with the /y/ sound. (worksheet 19.3)
3. Hand out magazines and other materials. Have the students cut out /y/ beginning sound pictures and glue them on a separate sheet of paper.

BLENDING

SKILL: Blend sounds together to make a word

MATERIALS: None

The following are /y/ words. The words are divided into two parts: the /y/ sound and the rest of the word. Pronounce each word to the children one part at a time (repeat three times for each word), and ask them to guess the word.

| y-ak | y-et | y-ellow |
| Y-ancy | y-es | |

SEGMENTATION

SKILL: Segment words into syllables

MATERIALS: The Yancy Yak story (worksheet 19.2)

Say /y/ words from the story and ask the children to clap one time for each word part.

    Young - 1 clap   Yancy - 2 claps
    Yak - 1 clap   Yard - 1 clap
    Yesterday - 3 claps   Yucky - 2 claps
    Yarn - 1 clap   Yummy - 2 claps

HOME ACTIVITY

SKILL: Identify the /y/ sound

MATERIALS: Worksheet 19.4, crayons, pencil

Parent instructs the child:

1. Take your pencil and trace the outline of Yancy Yak.
2. Color the picture of Yancy Yak.
3. What is this picture that begins with the /y/ sound?

/y/ as in Yak **155**

Yancy Yak

WORKSHEET 19.1

YANCY YAK

Young **Y**ancy **Y**ak played in the **y**ard **y**esterday. He played with a **y**ucky, **y**ellow ball of **y**arn. When he finished playing, **Y**ancy ate something **y**ummy. It was **y**ummy, **y**ellow **y**ogurt.

/y/ as in Yak 157

WORKSHEET 19.3

158 *Listening for Literacy*

Yancy Yak

WORKSHEET 19.4

CHAPTER 20

/w/ as in WALRUS

SOUND PRODUCTION

ACTIVITY 1

SKILL: Produce phoneme /w/ sound

MATERIALS: Mirror

The /w/ sound is voiced. The sound is made by forming the lips in a blowing shape. Have the students imitate you as you produce the sound. Turn on the motor and keep it running during production.

Have the children explore the shape of their mouths and placement of their lips as they make the /w/ sound. Have them feel their vocal folds for the phonation. Give each child a small hand mirror to observe the production of the sound. The /w/ sounds like wee, wee, wee.

ACTIVITY 2

SKILL: Repeat words beginning with the /w/ sound

MATERIALS: None

Model whole words that begin in the /w/ sound, and have the children repeat them.

Words that begin with /w/ include:

| water | wish |
| winter | work |

RHYMING

SKILL: Name two words that rhyme

MATERIALS: None

Share the following rhyme with the students. Have them listen very carefully and repeat back to you the first four lines.

>Wee Willie Winkie runs
>Through the town.
>Upstairs and downstairs,
>In his nightgown.

Ask the children to tell you the two words that rhyme. (town and gown)

Next, have the children listen to the whole rhyme.

>Wee Willie Winkie runs
>Through the town.
>Upstairs and downstairs,
>In his nightgown.
>Rapping at the window,
>Crying through the lock,
>Are the children in their beds?
>Now it's eight o'clock. (Mother Goose)

Ask the children for two rhyming words other than town and gown. (lock and clock)

AUDITORY DISCRIMINATION

SKILL: Discriminate the beginning sound of /w/

MATERIALS: None

Repeat the first pair of words below. Cover your mouth as the two words are pronounced. Have the students say "yes" if the words are the same, and "no" if they are not. Continue with the remaining pairs.

>wish and dish
>work and work

win and pin
was and was
wind and wind

INITIAL SOUND

ACTIVITY 1

SKILL: Discriminate beginning sound of /w/

MATERIALS: Wally Walrus worksheet 20.2

Introduce the Wally Walrus story. Read the story and ask the children to follow while listening for the words that begin with the /w/ phoneme. Read each sentence from the list below, and ask the children to say the words that begin with /w/.

1. Wally Walrus was walking down the street. (Wally, Walrus, was, walking)
2. He saw his friends Wendy and Wanda. (Wendy, Wanda)
3. They decided to walk to the store to look in the window. (walk, window)
4. They saw a wooly worm in the window. (wooly, worm, window)

ACTIVITY 2

SKILL: Identify /w/ beginning sounds in pictures and words

MATERIALS: Wally Walrus worksheets 20.1, 20.2, 20.3; magazines; scissors; glue; crayons; paper

Read the Wally Walrus story again, and ask the following questions:

1. What is the name of the walrus in the story?
2. Name some other things that begin with the /w/ sound. (worksheet 20.3)
3. Hand out magazines and other materials. Have the students cut out /w/ beginning sound pictures and glue them on a separate sheet of paper.

BLENDING

SKILL: Blend sounds together to make a word

MATERIALS: None

The following are /w/ words. The words are divided into two parts: the /w/ sound and the rest of the word. Pronounce each word to the children one part at a time (repeat three times for each word), and ask them to guess the word.

w-ater	W-anda	w-alk
w-alrus	W-ally	

SEGMENTATION

SKILL: Segment words into syllables

MATERIALS: The Wally Walrus story (worksheet 20.2)

Say /w/ words from the story and ask the children to clap one time for each word part.

Wally - 2 claps	Walrus - 2 claps
Walking - 2 claps	Wendy - 2 claps
Wanda - 2 claps	Walk - 1 clap
Wooly - 2 claps	Worm - 1 clap

HOME ACTIVITY

SKILL: Identify the /w/ sound

MATERIALS: Worksheet 20.4, crayons, pencil

Parent instructs the child:

1. Take your pencil and trace the outline of Wally Walrus.
2. Color the picture of Wally Walrus.
3. What is this picture that begins with the /w/ sound?

/w/ as in Walrus **163**

Wally Walrus

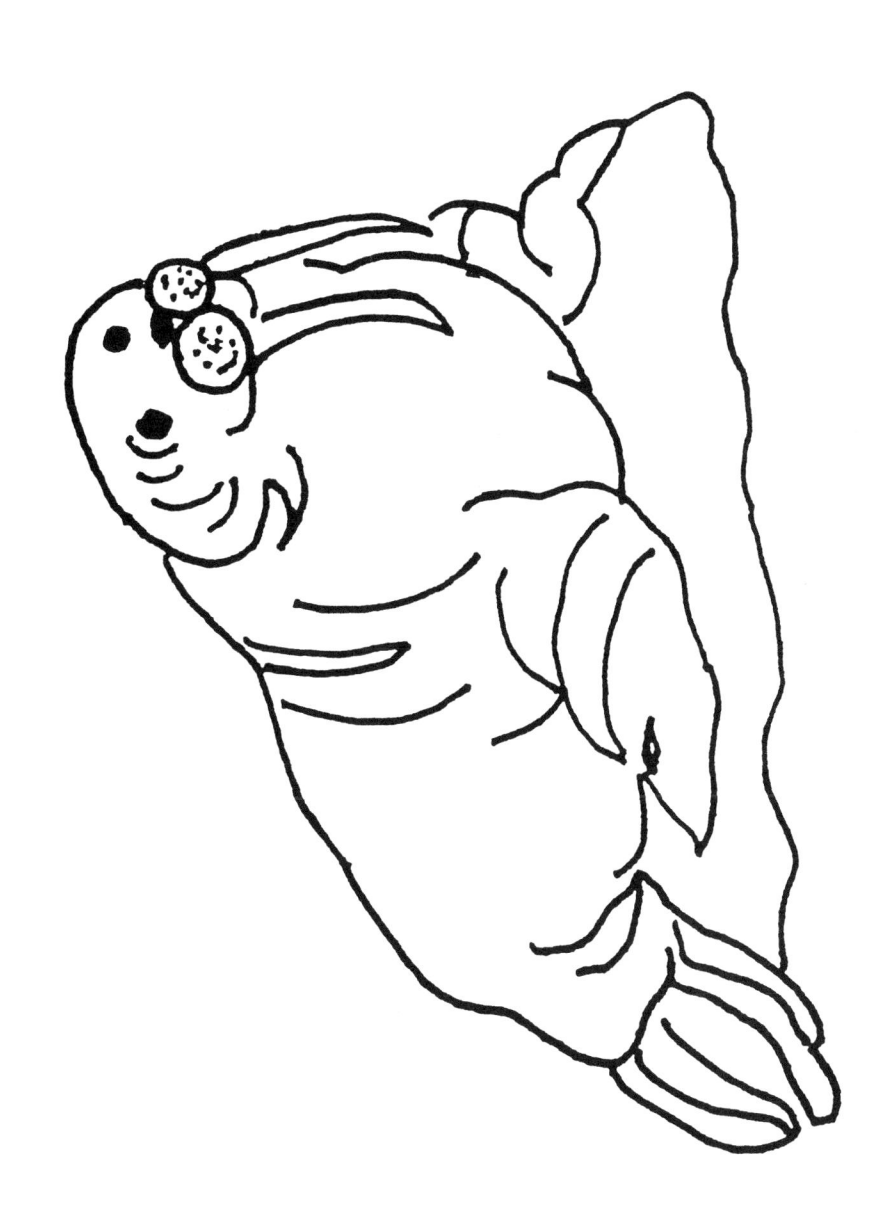

WORKSHEET 20.1

WALLY WALRUS

Wally Walrus was walking down the street. He saw his friends Wendy and Wanda. They decided to walk to the store to look in the window. They saw a wooly worm in the window.

WORKSHEET 20.2

/w/ as in Walrus   **165**

WORKSHEET 20.3

166 *Listening for Literacy*

Wally Walrus

WORKSHEET 20.4

CHAPTER 21

/h/ as in HIPPO

SOUND PRODUCTION

ACTIVITY 1

SKILL: Produce phoneme /h/ sound

MATERIALS: Mirror

The /h/ sound is unvoiced. A stream of breath is emitted through a narrow opening with some pressure, maintaining a continuous sound. There is no phonation.

Have the children explore the shape of their mouths as they make the /h/ sound. Give each child a small hand mirror to observe the production of the sound. Have the children open their mouths slightly and breathe into the mirror. The /h/ sounds like a panting dog.

ACTIVITY 2

SKILL: Repeat words beginning with the /h/ sound

MATERIALS: None

Model whole words that begin with the /h/ sound, and have the children repeat them.

Words that begin with /h/ include:

| happy | head | hug |
| hi | hair | |

RHYMING

SKILL: Name two words that rhyme

MATERIALS: None

Share the following rhyme with the students. Have them listen very carefully and repeat back to you the first two lines.

> Humpty Dumpty sat on a wall,
> Humpty Dumpty had a great fall

Ask the children to tell you the two words that rhyme. (wall and fall)

Next, have the children listen to the whole rhyme.

> Humpty Dumpty sat on a wall,
> Humpty Dumpty had a great fall,
> All the king's horses and all the king's men
> Couldn't put Humpty Dumpty together again.
> (Mother Goose)

Ask the children for two rhyming words other than wall and fall. (men and again)

AUDITORY DISCRIMINATION

SKILL: Discriminate the beginning sound of /h/

MATERIALS: None

Repeat the first pair of words below. Cover your mouth as the two words are pronounced. Have the students say "yes" if the words are the same, and "no" if they are not. Continue with remaining pairs.

> harp and carp
> hot and pot
> hippo and hippo
> hug and bug
> Harry and Harry

INITIAL SOUND

ACTIVITY 1

SKILL: Discriminate beginning sound of /h/

MATERIALS: Harry Hippo worksheet 21.2

Introduce the Harry Hippo story. Read the story and ask the children to follow while listening for the words that begin with the /h/ phoneme. Read each sentence from the list below, and ask the children to say the words that begin with /h/.

1. Harry Hippo is hungry. (Harry, Hippo, hungry)
2. He asks his mother for a hotdog and hot chocolate. (He, his, hotdog, hot)
3. Harry's mother says, "Harry, you must eat a hamburger today!" (Harry, hamburger)
4. Harry had a good lunch and hugged his mother. (Harry, had, hugged, his)

ACTIVITY 2

SKILL: Identify /h/ beginning sounds in pictures and words

MATERIALS: Harry Hippo worksheets 21.1, 21.2, 21.3; magazines; scissors; glue; crayons; paper

Read the Harry Hippo story again, and ask the following questions.

1. What is the name of the hippo in the story?
2. Name some other things that begin with the /h/ sound. (worksheet 21.3)
3. Hand out magazines and other materials. Have the students cut out /h/ beginning sound pictures and glue them on a separate sheet of paper.

BLENDING

SKILL: Blend sounds together to make a word

MATERIALS: None

The following are /h/ words. The words are divided into two parts: the /h/ sound and the rest of the word. Pronounce each word to the children one part at a time (repeat three times for each word), and ask them to guess the word.

| h-ippo | h-ip | h-ug |
| h-ot | H-arry | |

SEGMENTATION

SKILL: Segment words into syllables

MATERIALS: The Harry Hippo story (worksheet 21.2)

Say /h/ words from the story and ask the children to clap one time for each word part.

Harry - 2 claps	Hippo - 2 claps
Hotdog - 2 claps	Hot - 1 clap
Hamburger - 3 claps	Hugged - 1 clap

HOME ACTIVITY

SKILL: Identify the /h/ sound

MATERIALS: Worksheet 21.4, crayons, pencil

Parent instructs the child:

1. Take your pencil and trace the outline of Harry Hippo.
2. Color the picture of Harry Hippo.
3. What is this picture that begins with the /h/ sound?

/h/ as in Hippo **171**

Harry Hippo

WORKSHEET 21.1

HARRY HIPPO

Harry Hippo is hungry. He asks his mother for a hotdog and hot chocolate. Harry's mother says, "Harry, you must eat a hamburger today!" Harry had a good lunch and hugged his mother.

/h/ as in Hippo **173**

WORKSHEET 21.3

174   *Listening for Literacy*

Harry Hippo

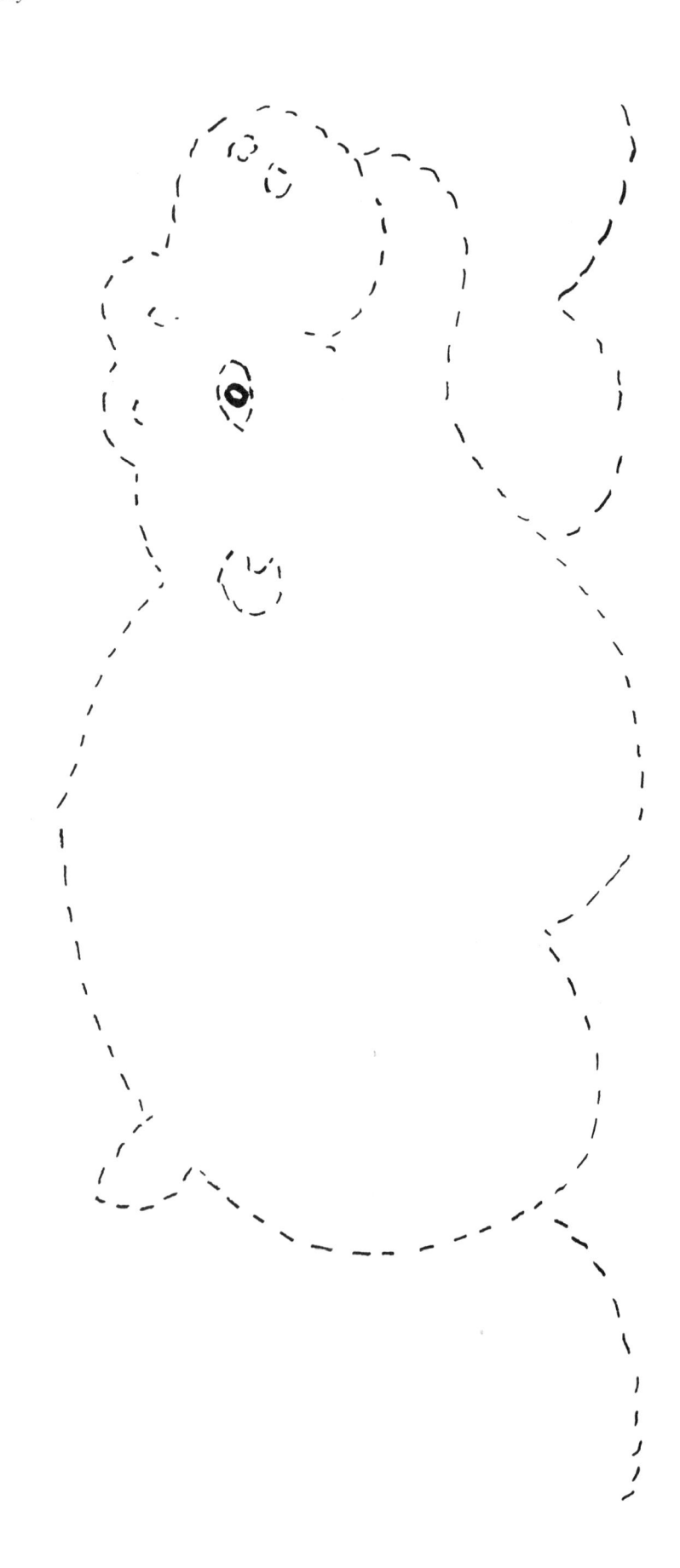

WORKSHEET 21.4

APPENDIX A

ACTIVITIES TO REINFORCE PHONEMIC AWARENESS

1. BILLY BAKER (Initial Sound activity)

   Billy Baker was a boy that put everything in his box that began with the same sound as Billy and Baker /b/. He put a banana, a buffalo and a bicycle in his box. Would he put a boat in his box? A peanut? A balloon? A kite? Ask the children to think of other things that Billy Baker would put in his big bix. The game can be played with other phonemes such as Kitty Kelly, Danny Dove, Mary Moore etc.

2. SAME SOUND AS NAMES (Initial Sound Activity)

   Suggest that children pretend that they like to do things or eat things that begin with the same sound as their names. Choose a child—Patty, for example, say, "Patty likes to paint pictures and eat pickles." What else would she like to do . . . pick poppies, play the piano, put pennies in her pocket, etc. Continue the activity with other children while the whole class participates in the guessing.

3. PHONEMIC CARD GAME (Phoneme awareness)

   Teacher prepares a pack of 3x5 cards each with an isolated phoneme. Dealer gives five cards to each player. Rest of the deck is placed face down in the center of the table. The top card is removed and placed face up beside the pack. The player sitting on the dealer's left arranges his cards without exposing them so he can see whether any two or more represent the same sound. He looks at the exposed card and says the sound of the phoneme and decides whether it matches with any in his hand. If not, he draws another card from the pack. If he has any matching cards, he places them on the table face up, saying the phonemes on his card. He discards one in his hand. The nex player to the left then goes through the same process of drawing, playing, and discarding. The procedure is repeated until one player has played or discarded all the cards in his hand.

4. SOUND GAME (Initial Sound Activity)

Teacher asks children to "listen" carefully for the first sound in a word. She calls out the word and the children raise their hands when they think they know which sound the word begins with.

5. I AM THINKING OF A WORD (Initial Sound Activity)

A list of words are written on the chalkboard. The teacher says, "I'm thinking of a word that begins with this sound (vowel or consonant phoneme), the children must guess which word it is from the list on the board.

6. SOUND BLENDING (Blending Activity)

Teacher will segment words of things around the classroom and ask the children to guess what object she was naming. Example: b-o-k (book) box, door, pencil, desk, ball, light, tablet, floor, ruler, girl, rope, map, window, flower, plant, chair, chalk, globe, crayons, pens, etc. Then the children take turns with segmenting by stretching out the word.

7. NAME GAME (blending activity)

   a. I see a girl named B_____.
   b. I see a girl named B-e-tt-y.
   c. I see a boy named J_____.
   d. I see a boy named J-o-n-y (Johnny).

8. WHAT'S MISSING?

Teacher uses pictures from a lotto game and omits the initial, medial, or final phoneme and asks the children to guess the word. _____ouse for house, cho_____late, tele_____one, fi_____, ig_____ for pig.

9. GUESSING ANIMALS, FRUITS, COLORS, etc.

   Teacher says, "We are going to pretend to be animals on a farm. We won't tell our full name only the beginning . . . I am a /p/____(pig). Play the same game with colors, fruits, etc.

10. PICTURE/PHONEME ID (Initial Sound)

    Teacher places a sheet with four pictures in front of the child. She names the pictures. Example: This is milk, a pumpkin, a banana, and a cat. Which picture begins with /m/ and teacher continues with the rest of the pictures.

APPENDIX B

PHONETIC SYMBOLS AND CLASSIFICATIONS OF AMERICAN ENGLISH CONSONANTS AND VOWELS

Table 1. American English consonant phonemes

Phonetic symbol	Phonic symbol	Graphemes for spelling
/p/	/p/	pit, spider, stop
/b/	/b/	bit, brat, bubble
/m/	/m/	mitt, slam, comb
/t/	/t/	tickle, stand, sipped
/d/	/d/	die, loved, handle
/n/	/n/	nice, knight, gnat
/k/	/k/	kite, crib, quiet, duck, walk
/g/	/g/	girl, Pittsburgh
/n/	/ng/	sing, bank, English
/f/	/f/	fluff, sphere, tough, calf
/v/	/v/	van, dove
/s/	/s/	psychic, pass, science, sit
/z/	/z/	jazz, xerox, zoo, cheese
/h/	/th/	think, breath, ether
/th/	/th/	this, breathe, either
/s/	/sh/	shoe, mission, sure
/z/	/zh/	measure, azure
/c/	/ch/	cheap, future, etch
/j/	/j/	judge, wage, residual
/l/	/l/	lamb, call, single
/r/	/r/	reach, singer, wrap, car
/y/	/y/	you, use, feud
/w/	/w/	witch, shower, queen
/w/	/wh/	where, when
/h/	/h/	house, who, rehab
Phonetic segment (allophone):		
/D/	t, J	writer, ladder, water

From Moats, L. C. (1995). *Spelling, development, disability, and instruction,* (p. 13) Timonium, MD: York Press; reprinted by permission.

Graphemes are spellings for individual phonemes; those in the word list are among the most common spellings, but the list does not include all possible graphemes for a given consonant.

180   Listening for Literacy

Table 2. American English consonants (phonic symbols)

	Lips	Lips/teeth	Tongue between teeth	Tongue behind teeth	Roof of mouth	Back of mouth	Throat
Stop	/p/			/t/		/k/	
	/b/			/d/		/g/	
Nasal	/m/			/n/		/ng/	
Fricative		/f/	/th/	/s/	/sh/		
		/v/	/th/	/z/	/zh/		
Affricate					/ch/		
					/j/		
Glide					/y/	/wh/	/h/
						/w/	
Liquid				/l/			
				/r/			

From Moats, L. C. (1995). *Spelling, development, disability, and instruction* (p. 12) Timonium, MD: York Press; reprinted by permission.

Table 3. American English vowels

Phonetic symbol	Phonic symbol	Spellings
/i/	ē	beet
/I/	i	bit
/e/	ā	bait
/e/	e	bet
/æ/	a	bat
/aj/	ī	bite
/a/	o	bottle
/ʌ/	u	butt
/c/	aw, ô	bought
/o/	ō	boat
/o/	oŏ	put
/u/	oō	boot
/e/	e	between
/cj/	oi, oy	boy
/æw/	ou, ow	bow

From Moats, L. C. (1995). *Spelling, development, disability, and instruction* (p. 17) Timonium, MD: York Press; reprinted by permission.

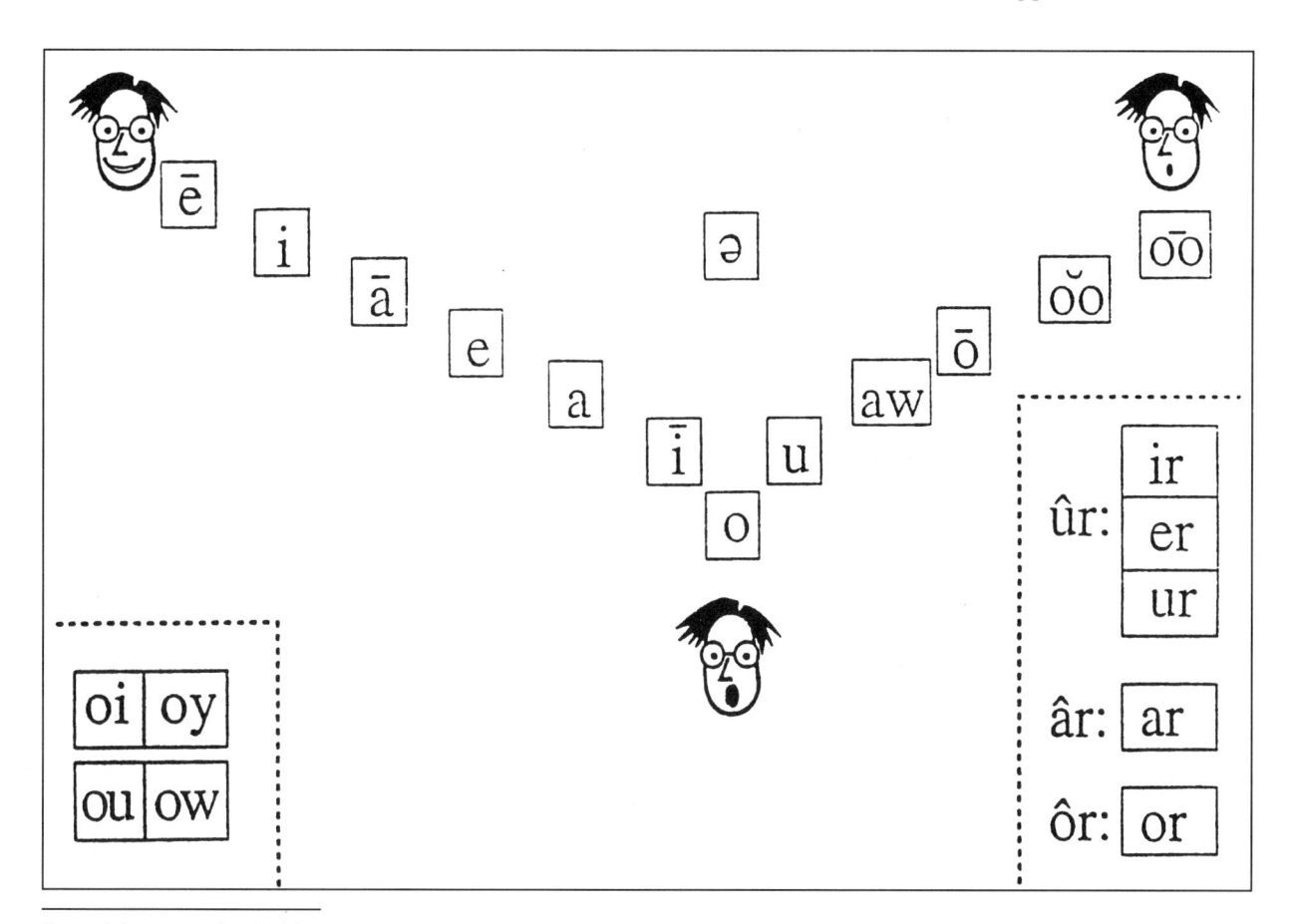

From Moats, L. C. (2000). *Speech to Print: Language Essentials for Teachers.* Baltimore, MD: Paul H. Brookes. Reprinted by permission.

Figure 1. Vowel spellings by mouth position.

APPENDIX C

SOUND ASSOCIATIONS FOR CREATING SOUND PERSONALITIES

/m/ humming or "/mmmm . . . mmmm/ good" sound from the Campbell's soup song

/p/ quiet motor boat or motor scooter sound

/b/ babbling brook, blowing bubbles, or "baa, baa" sheep sound

/w/ ceiling fan or "wee, wee, wee" (all the way home) little pig sound

/wh/ blowing sound (e.g., blowing out the birthday candles)

/h/ "ha, ha, ha" laughing or big sigh sound

/t/ ticking clock or metonome sound

/d/ pecking woodpecker or noisy tugboat enhine sound

/n/ neighing horse or maddening mosquito sound

/ng/ ringing bell sound (e.g., ding-dong)

/k/ coughing or cawing crow sound

/g/ emptying water jug or gurgling baby sound

/y/ yipping puppy or yipping coyote sound

/f/ mad cat or "fee-fie-foe-fum" beanstalk giant sound

/v/ big black fly sound

/sh/ "be quite" sound

/zh/ electric razor, hair clipper, or vacuum cleaner sound

/l/ "la-la-la" singing or humming telephone wire sound

183

IRVINE UNIFIED SCHOOL DISTRICT
FAMILY LITERACY PROJECT

Bibliography: K-3
Phonemic Awareness

Books

Title	Focuses on	Author
A Giraffe and a Half	rhyme	Silverstein, Shel
Alison's Zinnias	beginning sounds	Lobel, Anita
All "Dr. Seuss" books	rhyme	Dr. Seuss
Buzz Said the Bee	rhyme	Lewison, W.
Dinosaur Chase	rhyme	Otto, C.
Drummer Hoff	rhyme	Emberley, Barbara
I Can Fly	rhyme	Krauss, R.
I Love You, Good Night	rhyme	Buller, J. & Schade, S.
Is Your Mama a Llama?	rhyme	Guarino, Deborah
Jake Baked A Cake	rhyme	Hennessy, B. G.
Mother Goose Nursery Rhymes	rhyme	
Pass the Fritters, Critters	rhyme	Chapman, Cheryl
Possum Come a-Knockin'	rhyme	Van Lann, Nancy
Rachel Fister's Blister	rhyme	MacDonald, Amy
Silly Sally	rhyme	Wood, Audry
Sing a Song of Popcorn	rhyme	Beatrice Schenk de Regniers
Six Sleepy Sheep	rhyme	Gordon, J.
Stop That Noise!	rhyme	Geraghty, P.
The Rooster Crows	rhyme	Maude and Miska Petersham
The Random House Book of Poetry for Children	rhyme	J. Prelutsky
Tomie de Paola's Mother Goose	rhyme	T. De Paola
Who Is Tapping at My Window?	rhyme	Deming, A. G.

Songs

Title	Focuses on	
Any "Raffi" songs	multiple areas	
Any "Wee Sing Silly Songs"	multiple areas	
Apples and Bananas	rhyme	
Down by the Bay	rhyme	
Spider on the Floor	rhyme	
Willaby Wallaby Woo	rhyme	

Source: Teaching Phonics, Phonemic Awareness, and Word Recognition. Bishop, Ashley, & Suzanne, Teacher Created Materials, Inc., 1996.

Websites

"Materials to Teach Phonemic Awareness. . ."
http://www.ldonline.org/ld_indepth/teaching_techniques/materials.html

CEC "Tips for Teachers"
http://www.cec.sped.org/cricex/ttips.htm

"Beginning Reading and Phonological Awareness for Students . . ."
http://www.ldonline.org/ld_indepth/reading/eric540.html

"Early Language Intervention Activity Starters . . ."
http://www.audiospeech.ubc.ca/eli/elikern.htm

"Learning to Read, Reading to Learn . . ."
http://www.edc.org/NECAC/resources/l-ttips.html

"Lexia Phonics-Based REading Software"
http://www.lexialearning.com/phonics.html

"Building a Powerful Reading Program . . ."
http://www.ksagrop.com/thecenter/build_read/3.html

"Welcome to Letterland"
http://www.letterland.com/

"Academic Interventions for Children with Dylexia . . ."
http://kidsource.com/kidsource/content2/dyslexia.html

"Sound Companion"
http://www.linguisystems.com/exsogame.htm

"Kid Source Speech & Language Milestone Chart & Activities"
http://kidsource.com/LDA/speech_language.html

"Bridge to Reading"
http://www.wolfenet.com/~por/index.html

"Phonological Awareness Training for Reading"
http://www.accesspoints.com/pro-ed/patr.html

"Phonological Awareness: Curricular and Instructional Implications"
http://darkwing.uoregon.edu/~ncite/Reading/PhonoImp.html

Teaching Exceptional Children: A Learner's Permit to the World Wide Web
http://www.nscee.edu/unlv.Colleges/Education/Erc/contents.html
- TEC on line. Contents page with links to all articles in the May '98 volume featuring a variety of articles on the web

Council for Exceptional Children
http://www.cec.sped.org
- Council for Exceptional Children. Links to Divisions, Federations & Special Education info.

Learning Disabilities on line
http://ldonline.org/
- Excellent resources for parents, teachers, students. Focus on LD.

Special Education Technology
http://www.ed.sc.edu/caw/toolboxat.html
- Links to vendors for educational software and assistive technology.

Seussville: The Sneetches
http://randomhousel.com/seussville/games.sneetches/game.html
- Memory and ordering of the patterns of stars.

Webaphabet by NET TECH
http://sagan.enc.org/workshop/webphabet/wbet.htm
- An online, interactive alphabet for pre-readers and beginning readers (Kids from K–2).

Kidpix
http://www.learningco.com
- Children can draw and point. Tools for creating and exploring.

Earobics
http://www.cogcon.com
- Interactive games for pre-readers, Auditory Discrimination, Sequencing, and Memory.

Bailey's Book House
http://www.edmark.com
- Interactive games for ages 2–5. Rhymes, story writing. Fun to play.

Auburn University
http://www.auburn.edu/~murraba/assess.html
- Assessing Phonimic Awareness.

Eric on line
http://ericec.ort
- Lots of information on reading, phonological and phonemic awareness.

Pictures
http://www.geocities.com
- Parthenon picture.

Crayola
http://education.crayola.com/lessons
- Pictures.

International site
http://www.tesan.vuurwerk.nl/diaroes/t2/index.htm
- Great pictures.

References

Ball, E. W., & Blachman, B. S. (1988). Phoneme segmentation training. Effect on reading readiness. *Annuals of Dyslexia, 38,* 208–225.

Chard, D. J., & Dickson, S. V. (1999). Phonological awareness: Instructional and assessment guidelines. *Intervention in School and Clinic, 34,* 261–270.

Edelen-Smith, P. (1999). How now brown cow: phoneme awareness activities for collaborative classrooms. *Intervention in School and Clinic, 33,* 103–111, Pro-Ed., Inc.

Ehri, K. C., & Wilce, L. S. (1980). The influence of orthography on readers' conceptualization of the phonemic structure of words. *Applied Psycholinguistics, 1,* 371–385.

Goswami, U. (1994). Phonological skills, analogies, and reading development. *Reading Behavior, US,* 32–37.

Juel, C. (1991). Beginning Reading. In R. Barr, M. L. Kamil, P. B. Mosenthal, & P. D. Peaarson (eds.), Handbook of Reading Research (V2, pp. 750–7898). New York: Longman.

Juel, C. (1988). Learning to read and write: A longitudinal study of 54 children from first through fourth grades. *Journal of Educational Psychology, 80,* 437–447.

Lewkowicz, N. K. (1980). Phonemic awareness training: What to teach and how to teach it. *Journal of Educational Psychology, 72,* 686–700.

Lundberg, I., Frost, J., & Peterson, O. P. (1988). Effects of an extensive program for stimulating phonological awareness in preschool children. *Reading Research Quarterly, 23,* 274–284.

Libermanm I. Y. Shankweiler, D., Fischer, F. W. & Carter, B. (1974). Explicit syllable and phoneme segemtnation in the young child. *Journal of Experimental Child Psychology, 18,* 201–212.

O'Connor, R. E., Jenkins, J. R., Leicester, N., & Slocum, T. A. (1993). Teaching phonological awareness to young children with learning disabilities. *Exceptional Children, 59,* 532–547.

Perfetti, C. A., Beck, I., Bell, L. & Hughes, C. (1987). Phonemic knowledge and learning to read are reciprocal: A longitudinal study of first grade children. *Merrill-Palmer Quarterly, 33,* 283–319.

Snow, C. E. Burns, M. S. & Griffin, P. (Eds.). (1998). Preventing Reading Difficulties in Youn Children. Washington, DC. National Academy Press.

Strickland, D., & Cullinan, B. C. (1990). Afterwoord. In M. J. Adams, Beginning to read: Thinking and learning about pring (pp. 425–434). Cambridge, MA: MIT Press.

Wagner, R. K., Torgensen, J. K., Laughon, P., Simmons, K., & Rashotte, C. (1993). The development of young readers' phonological processing abilities. *Journal of Educational Psychology, 85,* 83–103.